Tides and currents

Tides and currents

David Arnold

Fernhurst Books

First published 1986 by
Fernhurst Books, 53 High Street, Steyning, W. Sussex

ISBN 0 906754 24 0

Acknowledgements
Figures 1.2, 1.4 and 1.6 are reproduced by kind permission of the publishers of *The Macmillan and Silk Cut Nautical Almanac*. Figures 1.1, 1.4, 1.5, 1.6, 1.7, 1.8, 5.1, 5.8, 6.4, and 6.5 are Crown copyright and are based upon British Admiralty Charts with the permission of the Controller of HM Stationery Office and of the Hydrographer of the Navy. The photographs are by Roger Lean-Vercoe.

Composition by A & G Phototypesetters, Knaphill
Printed by Ebenezer Baylis & Son Ltd, Worcester

Contents

1 Predicting the tides   7
2 Local effects   18
3 Basic tidal tactics   22
4 Racing on the Olympic triangle   31
5 Inshore racing   42
6 Offshore racing   51
7 Tide facts   59

ENGLAND, SOUTH COAST - PORTSMOUTH

LAT 50°48'N   LONG 1°07'W

TIMES AND HEIGHTS OF HIGH AND LOW WATERS

TIME ZONE GMT
For Summer Time add ONE hour in tinted area

JANUARY

Day	Time / M	Time / M	Time / M	Time / M
1 SA	0016 4.8	0526 0.8	1232 4.8	1754 0.5
2 SU	0105 4.8	0614 0.9	1319 4.7	1841 0.6
3 M	0155 4.8	0703 1.0	1406 4.6	1930 0.8
4 TU	0248 4.7	0754 1.2	1458 4.5	2022 1.0
5 W	0343 4.6	0849 1.4	1553 4.3	2119 1.2
6 TH	0441 4.4	0950 1.5	1657 4.1	2221 1.4
7 F	0543 4.2	1058 1.6	1807 3.9	2331 1.6
8 SA	0648 4.1	1210 1.6	1922 3.9	
9 SU	0041 1.6	0751 4.1	1316 1.5	2030 3.9
10 M	0142 1.6	0845 4.2	1412 1.4	2124 4.1
11 TU	0233 1.5	0934 4.3	1500 1.3	2211 4.2
12 W	0316 1.4	1017 4.4	1541 1.1	2252 4.3
13 TH	0356 1.2	1057 4.4	1619 1.0	2328 4.4
14 F	0432 1.1	1133 4.4	1652 1.0	
15 SA	0003 4.3	0507 1.1	1207 4.3	1726 0.9
16 SU	0035 4.3	0540 1.1	1241 4.3	1758 0.9
17 M	0109 4.3	0614 1.1	1314 4.2	1830 0.9
18 TU	0145 4.3	0647 1.2	1348 4.2	1903 0.9
19 W	0220 4.3	0722 1.2	1424 4.1	1939 1.0
20 TH	0258 4.3	0757 1.3	1502 4.1	2016 1.1
21 F	0337 4.2	0838 1.4	1545 4.0	2101 1.3
22 SA	0421 4.1	0929 1.5	1637 3.9	2159 1.5
23 SU	0516 3.9	1034 1.6	1744 3.8	2309 1.6
24 M	0624 4.0	1150 1.6	1901 3.9	
25 TU	0027 1.6	0737 4.1	1306 1.4	2017 4.1
26 W	0139 1.4	0845 4.3	1413 1.1	2124 4.3
27 TH	0241 1.1	0947 4.5	1513 0.9	2223 4.5
28 F	0337 0.9	1044 4.6	1606 0.6	2317 4.7
29 SA	0428 0.7	1135 4.7	1655 0.4	
30 SU	0006 4.8	0516 0.7	1222 4.8	1742 0.5
31 M	0054 4.8	0602 0.7	1306 4.7	1827 0.5

FEBRUARY

Day	Time / M	Time / M	Time / M	Time / M
1 TU	0140 4.9	0648 0.8	1351 4.7	1912 0.6
2 W	0227 4.8	0732 0.9	1436 4.6	1956 0.8
3 TH	0313 4.7	0818 1.1	1523 4.4	2044 1.0
4 F	0359 4.5	0908 1.3	1616 4.2	2136 1.3
5 SA	0452 4.2	1006 1.5	1717 3.9	2239 1.7
6 SU	0552 4.0	1117 1.7	1834 3.7	2354 1.9
7 M	0702 3.8	1236 1.7	1955 3.7	
8 TU	0111 1.9	0813 3.9	1346 1.6	2104 3.8
9 W	0213 1.7	0913 4.0	1442 1.4	2157 4.0
10 TH	0302 1.5	1001 4.1	1526 1.2	2238 4.1
11 F	0342 1.3	1043 4.2	1603 1.1	2313 4.3
12 SA	0417 1.1	1118 4.3	1636 0.9	2343 4.3
13 SU	0450 1.0	1149 4.3	1707 0.8	
14 M	0013 4.4	0523 0.9	1220 4.3	1739 0.7
15 TU	0045 4.4	0555 0.9	1253 4.3	1812 0.7
16 W	0120 4.4	0629 0.8	1327 4.3	1844 0.6
17 TH	0156 4.4	0659 0.8	1403 4.3	1917 0.7
18 F	0231 4.4	0732 0.9	1440 4.3	1951 0.8
19 SA	0307 4.3	0807 1.0	1519 4.1	2029 1.0
20 SU	0347 4.2	0852 1.2	1606 4.0	2120 1.3
21 M	0438 4.0	0952 1.5	1710 3.8	2231 1.6
22 TU	0548 3.8	1114 1.6	1836 3.7	
23 W	0001 1.7	0712 3.9	1245 1.5	2004 3.9
24 TH	0125 1.5	0830 4.1	1402 1.2	2115 4.2
25 F	0233 1.2	0935 4.3	1503 0.8	2215 4.4
26 SA	0328 0.9	1032 4.5	1556 0.5	2306 4.7
27 SU	0417 0.7	1122 4.6	1643 0.3	2353 4.8
28 M	0503 0.5	1207 4.7	1727 0.3	

MARCH

Day	Time / M	Time / M	Time / M	Time / M
1 TU	0037 4.9	0547 0.5	1250 4.8	1810 0.4 (boxed)
2 W	0120 4.9	0627 0.6	1331 4.7	1849 0.5
3 TH	0200 4.8	0707 0.7	1413 4.7	1927 0.7
4 F	0239 4.7	0746 0.9	1455 4.5	2007 1.0
5 SA	0318 4.4	0828 1.2	1539 4.2	2052 1.4
6 SU	0400 4.2	0917 1.5	1632 3.9	2147 1.7
7 M	0454 3.9	1022 1.7	1741 3.6	2303 2.0
8 TU	0608 3.7	1147 1.9	1912 3.5	
9 W	0033 2.0	0733 3.6	1313 1.8	2035 3.6
10 TH	0150 1.8	0847 3.7	1418 1.6	2133 3.8
11 F	0244 1.6	0941 3.9	1504 1.3	2215 4.1
12 SA	0324 1.3	1022 4.1	1539 1.0	2249 4.3
13 SU	0356 1.2	1055 4.2	1611 0.6	2318 4.4
14 M	0427 0.9	1125 4.3	1642 0.7	2347 4.5
15 TU	0458 0.9	1155 4.4	1715 0.6	
16 W	0018 4.5	0531 0.7	1228 4.4	1750 0.5
17 TH	0053 4.5	0605 0.6	1304 4.5	1822 0.5
18 F	0128 4.6	0637 0.6	1342 4.3	1856 0.5
19 SA	0205 4.5	0711 0.6	1421 4.4	1929 0.7
20 SU	0243 4.4	0746 0.8	1502 4.2	2007 1.0
21 M	0323 4.2	0830 1.1	1549 4.0	2058 1.3
22 TU	0405 3.9	0930 1.4	1655 3.8	2212 1.6
23 W	0529 3.7	1056 1.6	1828 3.5	2349 1.7
24 TH	0701 3.7	1233 1.5	1959 3.8	
25 F	0118 1.5	0821 3.9	1350 1.2	2107 4.2
26 SA	0223 1.2	0924 4.2	1449 0.9	2202 4.5
27 SU	0316 0.9	1016 4.4	1539 0.5	2249 4.7
28 M	0401 0.7	1102 4.6	1625 0.3	2332 4.8
29 TU	0444 0.5	1146 4.7	1707 0.3	
30 W	0015 4.9	0525 0.5	1228 4.8	1747 0.5
31 TH	0054 4.9	0603 0.5	1310 4.7	1824 0.5

APRIL

Day	Time / M	Time / M	Time / M	Time / M
1 F	0131 4.8	0639 0.6	1349 4.6	1858 0.8
2 SA	0205 4.7	0714 0.8	1428 4.5	1931 1.1
3 SU	0238 4.5	0751 1.1	1507 4.2	2010 1.4
4 M	0316 4.2	0835 1.4	1554 3.9	2101 1.8
5 TU	0405 3.9	0932 1.7	1655 3.7	2212 2.0
6 W	0513 3.6	1051 2.0	1822 3.5	2346 2.1
7 TH	0644 3.4	1224 1.9	1950 3.5	
8 F	0111 1.9	0807 3.5	1337 1.7	2054 3.8
9 SA	0211 1.6	0905 3.8	1427 1.4	2138 4.0
10 SU	0252 1.3	0948 4.0	1504 1.1	2214 4.3
11 M	0325 1.1	1022 4.2	1538 0.9	2245 4.5
12 TU	0356 0.9	1053 4.4	1612 0.7	2316 4.6
13 W	0427 0.8	1125 4.5	1647 0.6	2347 4.7
14 TH	0502 0.6	1201 4.6	1723 0.5	
15 F	0023 4.7	0538 0.5	1241 4.6	1800 0.5
16 SA	0101 4.7	0615 0.5	1322 4.5	1834 0.6
17 SU	0141 4.6	0652 0.6	1405 4.4	1912 0.8
18 M	0222 4.4	0733 0.7	1452 4.3	1955 1.1
19 TU	0308 4.2	0821 1.0	1545 4.0	2050 1.4
20 W	0405 3.9	0924 1.3	1655 3.8	2208 1.7
21 TH	0522 3.7	1051 1.5	1826 3.8	2342 1.7
22 F	0652 3.7	1220 1.4	1949 4.0	
23 SA	0104 1.5	0809 3.9	1332 1.1	2052 4.2
24 SU	0206 1.2	0907 4.2	1428 0.8	2141 4.5
25 M	0256 0.9	0955 4.4	1516 0.6	2225 4.7
26 TU	0339 0.7	1039 4.6	1601 0.5	2307 4.8
27 W	0421 0.6	1121 4.7	1643 0.5	2347 4.8
28 TH	0500 0.5	1206 4.7	1721 0.6	
29 F	0025 4.8	0537 0.6	1248 4.6	1756 0.7
30 SA	0023 4.7	0611 0.6	1327 4.5	1828 0.9

Chart Datum: 2.74 metres below Ordnance Datum (Newlyn)

1 Predicting the tides

Simple tide tables and diagrams were in existence for many ports from the year 1200 AD onwards. People were convinced by observation that there was an association between the moon and the observed level of the water. Later, it was realised that the sun had a smaller but noticeable effect on tides.

The detailed explanation of the causes of tides, why they vary in duration and why they change in period in various parts of the earth, is given in the last chapter of this book. For now, a short list of definitions will help you understand the terminology used both in this book and in other books you will need to refer to.

Tide. This refers to the periodical vertical oscillation of the sea in response to the tide-generating forces of the moon and the sun. Note that it is the *vertical* oscillation – compare with the next definition.

Tidal stream. This is the periodical *horizontal* oscillation of the sea in response to the tide-generating forces of the moon and the sun.

Current. This refers to horizontal movement of the water that is due to causes *other* than the tide-generating forces of the moon and the sun. These causes are mainly meteorological (such as wind drift) or geographical (rivers, headlands and the like).

Waterflow. This is the horizontal effect felt by the sailor, and is a combination of the tidal stream and the current at any point.

Predicting the tides

It should be remembered that although tides vary with geographical effects and meteorological conditions, they are predictable to within reasonably fine limits. It is important to get the basic predictions right and the tools of the trade for this exercise are as follows:

- Tide tables.
- A tidal atlas.
- A chart with indications of tide on it.

Of the above, tide tables are essential in all cases, whereas a tidal atlas is more use for inshore races and a chart more use for offshore races.

Tide tables

In practically every country where sailing takes place, tide tables are available giving the daily times and heights of the tide. Hydrographic departments produce official tide tables but yachtsmen more often use commercial or specialist almanacs which contain tidal information for the country concerned, together with tidal stream charts (small atlases) and notes on the peculiarities of the tide in certain areas. Most almanacs also contain an explanation of tides in general and how to use the tidal section of the particular almanac in question. It is very important to obtain adequate tide tables for the race area and to have a chance to study them before the race begins.

We now look at how to read tide tables, and from them predict the depth of water at any one time in the area concerned. We must also extract from the tide tables times of high and low water on the day in question, and ascertain whether the tides are at springs or at neaps (see chapter 7). From this it is possible to use your tidal atlas (or the diamonds on the chart, if racing offshore) to predict the tidal stream.

How to read tide tables

The predictions for Portsmouth on the south coast of England are reproduced in figure 1.1. All the examples in this chapter are taken from this figure so you will be able to follow the working from the primary source of information.

Portsmouth, being a large commercial port, is known as a *standard port* which has its own predictions. The smaller, less important ports rely on the predictions for standard ports with similar characteristics (usually nearby, but not always). In the example given later, the standard port is Portsmouth and the secondary port is Cowes (on the Isle of Wight). Corrections for time and depth are applied to the predictions for the standard port to give the predictions for the secondary port. More of this later.

Information given

Look now at the example in figure 1.1 for Portsmouth. The months are given at the top of the page and the dates run down in heavy type (with an abbreviation for the day of the week underneath) in two columns for each month. You will see that on the top left of the page the time zone is in Greenwich Mean Time (GMT) and all times on the page are given in this time. The tinted area (which begins at about midnight on 27 March) represents the introduction of British Summer Time. This means that one hour must be added to all the predictions in the tinted area.

Have a look at 1 March (Tuesday). The first time given is 0037 (37 minutes past midnight in the morning) and a high water is shown of 4.9 metres. The next tide is at 0547 which shows a low water of 0.5 metres. Both of these are heights above the *chart datum* (see below). Later in the day at 1250, another high water (though slightly lower than the first) of 4.8 metres is shown, and in the evening at 1810 (6:10 p.m.) another low

water of 0.4 metres is shown. From these figures can be derived several pieces of information which are outlined below. Write down the times and heights horizontally across the page of your notebook.

If we move on to 1 April (which is in the tinted zone) the relevant times in British Summer Time are one hour more than those shown in the tide tables. On 1 April, therefore, the times should be noted as 0231, 0739, 1449 and 1958. The heights opposite the original times remain as before, since they are unaffected by adjustment of the clocks for Summer Time. The example given is from the *Macmillan and Silk Cut Nautical Almanac* but there are tide tables that allow for the addition of Summer Time. This is confusing, and so it is essential to check at the top of the page the time to which the tides are related.

Chart datum

Both the chart and the tide tables are based on a datum level, which is approximately the level of the *lowest astronomical spring tide* (pretty well the lowest the tide is going to get without exceptional weather conditions). Figure 1.2 shows various definitions; note that chart datum is shown by the heavy line near the bottom of the figure.

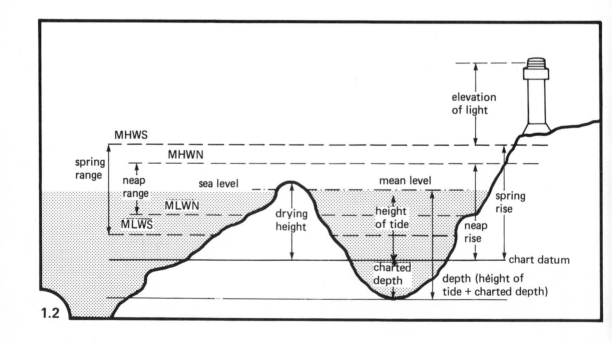

1.2

Charted depth

Modern almanacs show the rise of the tide above chart datum in metres. Most charts show the depth in any one place above chart datum in metres too. Adding the rise of tide to the charted depth will give the depth at the time concerned.

For example, on 1 March at 1250 in a place where the charted depth is 3 metres, the rise of tide is shown as 4.8 metres. The depth is found by adding the *height of tide* (rise of tide) to the *charted depth*, namely 7.8 metres (4.8 + 3 metres).

When looking at a chart, make sure that the depth is shown in metres and tenths of a metre. Some of the older charts are still shown in fathoms and feet. Since a fathom is approximately twice as big as a metre this makes a very big difference!

Duration

This is the time between the prediction of high water and low water and is usually about six and a quarter hours. The duration is very important for working out the intermediate heights between high and low water. On 1 March the duration between high and low water is 5 hrs 10 mins in the first instance (0547 minus 0037); later in the day this increases to 5 hrs 20 mins (1810 minus 1250).

Range

Range is the difference between the given height for low water and the given height of high water. It is maximum at spring tides (when the low water is lower and the high water is higher) and minimum at neap tides (when the difference between high and low water is least). Going back to our example of 1 March, the first range is 4.4 metres (4.9 metres HW minus 0.5 metres LW) and the second range is also 4.4 metres (4.8 metres HW minus 0.4 metres LW).

Springs and neaps

The explanation for springs and neaps is given in chapter 7. By looking at the tide tables and comparing the heights for a period of two weeks, the combination of the highest high waters and lowest low waters can be found (i.e. the greatest range), and you can then put an 'S' (for springs) alongside. When high waters are lowest and low waters highest (i.e. the smallest range) put an 'N' alongside for neaps. Having filled these in it is an easy matter to find out whether the race dates will coincide with springs or neaps. (A more formal way of doing this is to plot the ranges over two weeks).

Reference to the period around 1 March in figure 1.1 will show that on 1 March Portsmouth experienced a spring tide with a range of 4.4 metres. The preceding neaps were on Wednesday 23 February (in the morning the range was only 2.2 metres) and after 1 March, neaps occurred again on 9 March with a range of only 1.6 metres in the morning. This confirms the fortnightly pattern of springs and neaps described in chapter 7.

Armed with range, duration, and a knowledge of the state of the tide (quarter springs, half springs, three-quarter springs or neaps) you can now go forward to your depth predictions.

Using the tide tables to predict depth of water

There are three methods used to predict the depth of water (rise of tide) at any time. These are (in ascending order of accuracy):

- The rule of twelfths.
- The standard diagram for tidal interpolation.
- Tidal curves for a specific port.

Rule of twelfths

This is a very rough rule and is mainly intended for use at times of stress (for example in the middle of a race) when an approximate calculation is required in a hurry. You divide the range by 12 and then assume that in the first hour of the tide the rise (or fall) will be 1/12th, the second hour it will be 2/12s, the third and fourth hours it will be 3/12s, the fifth hour 2/12ths again and the last hour 1/12th again (this assumes a six-hour rise and fall). From figure 1.3 it can be seen that the method approximates to a sine curve and it certainly has its uses.

> **Example 1**
> *Find the rise of tide at 1520 GMT on 1 March at Portsmouth*
> Range = 4.4 metres
> HW = 1250
> One-twelfth of range = 4.4 ÷ 12 = 0.37 metre
> Time required = 1520 (2½ hrs after HW)
> Fall of tide = $0.37 + (2 \times 0.37) + \frac{1}{2}(3 \times 0.37)$
>   1st hr   2nd hr   3rd ½hr
>   = $4\frac{1}{2} \times 0.37$
>   = 1.67 m
> HW − fall = $4.80 - 1.67$
>   = 3.13 metres
>
> The height of tide at 1520 GMT is 3.13 metres.

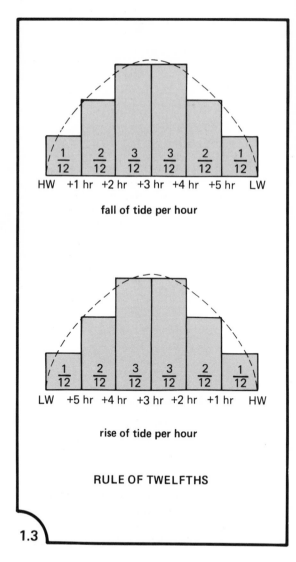

fall of tide per hour

rise of tide per hour

RULE OF TWELFTHS

1.3

Standard diagram

Figure 1.4 can be used where no special curve has been drawn for the port concerned. This figure also approximates to a sine curve, but allows for the duration of the tide instead of assuming (as in the rule of twelfths) a six-hour duration in all cases.

Starting with the time before (or after) high water (horizontal scale), read down the graph to the relevant duration curve to obtain a factor which turns out to be a percentage of the range which will have occurred at that particular time. Next, take the range, multiply it by the factor and add the result to low water to give the height above chart datum. This method also works in reverse if required, because for a given depth one can predict the time that that depth will be achieved. This is useful if you need to know the time you can enter or leave a tidal port, or – if you are aground – the time you should refloat. An example is given opposite.

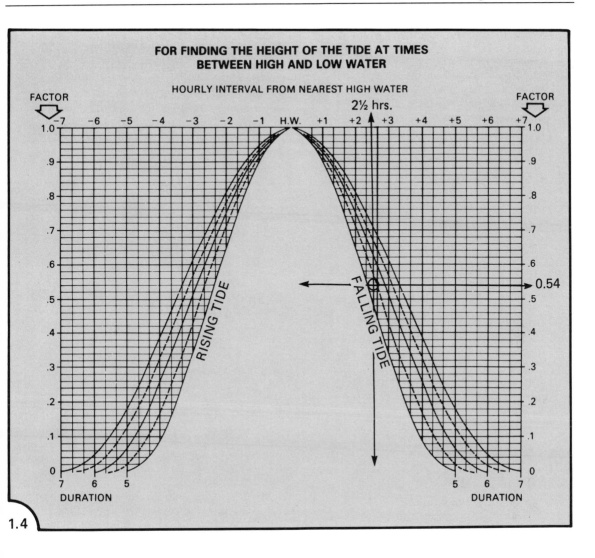

FOR FINDING THE HEIGHT OF THE TIDE AT TIMES BETWEEN HIGH AND LOW WATER

1.4

Example 2 – Standard curves

Find the rise of tide at 1520 GMT on 1 March at Portsmouth

Range = 4.40 metres
Duration = 5hr 20mins
Falling tide
Time 1520 is 2½ hr after HW at 1250

From figure 1.4 the factor is 0.54
Rise of tide = range × factor
   = 4.40 × 0.54
   = 2.38 metres

Rise + LW = 2.38 + 0.40
   = 2.78 metres

The height of tide at 1520 GMT is 2.78 metres (i.e about 35 cm below the result in example 1).

The standard diagram in figure 1.4 will be omitted from the *Macmillan and Silk Cut Nautical Almanac* after the 1986 edition, although it may appear in other publications for some years yet.

As tidal predictions improve, standard specific diagrams for each major port will be incorporated in tide tables; the method of use for the latest variant of these is detailed below.

Tidal curves for a specific port

Shown in figure 1.5 are the curves drawn specifically for Portsmouth. These are the new curves which appear in the *Admiralty Tide Tables* for 1986. Separate curves are shown for springs and neaps. The method of use is as follows.

Example 3 – Specific curves

Find the height of tide at Portsmouth on 1 March at 1520, tide falling.
1   Plot LW on the bottom line in figure 1.5 (0.4 metres).
2   Plot HW on the top line (4.8 metres at 1250 on 1 March).
3   Join these two points up.
4   Plot in the time of HW and subsequent hours during the afternoon. Between 1450 and 1550,

run the 1520 line vertically upward to the appropriate curve (in this case the spring tide curve, since the range of 4.0 metres is above the spring range shown on the figure of 4.1 metres), at point A.
5   From A, draw a horizontal line to the HW/LW line (step 3) to intersect at point B.
6   Draw a line vertically up from B to the range scale, and read the height of tide, which is 3.82 metres at Portsmouth at 1520 on 1 March.

Note that the process may be reversed to find the time that a certain height is predicted. Start from the top line at the height of tide, go vertically down to B on the diagonal line, then horizontally across to the appropriate curve, then vertically down to the time at which that height is expected.

Where specific tidal curves such as the above are available, they should always be used, as they are by far the most accurate way to work out tidal heights or times.

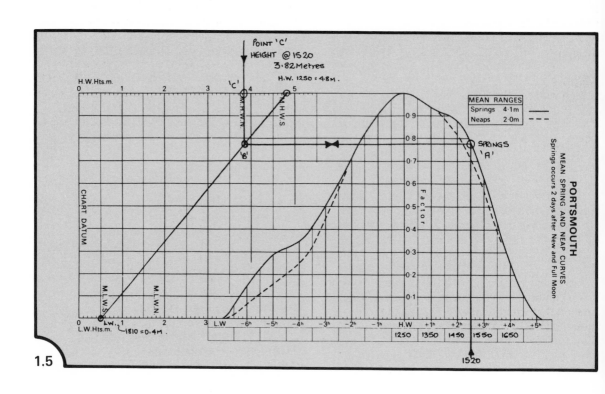

1.5

It will be noted that the rise of tide using the specific curves is over a metre more than that shown in Example 2. This is because of the double high water in the Solent (shown on the spring curve as a high water, followed by a lower 'high water' at about 1 hr 40 mins after the first one). From then on the tide falls fairly rapidly. Nonetheless, this means that there is a 'stand' of tide which distorts the standard curve into these specific curves. This is why it is so important to use the specific curves for a port.

Secondary ports

Figure 1.6 shows the information given for Cowes on the Isle of Wight. This can be applied to the predictions for Portsmouth to give predictions for Cowes. To do this we need to interpolate values.

Interpolation
Interpolation is a method of estimating an intermediate value. We do this all the time in everyday life; if 5 litres of paint cost £5, we expect 1 litre to cost £1; if it takes the bath four minutes to fill we are happy to turn on the taps and leave the room for a couple of minutes – and would be surprised if the tub wasn't half-full when we got back. Interpolating tidal time and height differences operates in just the same way.

Heights
If high water at Portsmouth is 4.7 metres (top row in the table in figure 1.6) then the height at Cowes (from the 'Difference row) is 0.5 metres less than that, i.e. 4.2 metres. If HW Portsmouth is 3.8, then height at Cowes is 0.3 less than that, i.e. 3.5 metres. If HW Portsmouth falls between these values, then the amount to be subtracted for the Cowes height will be in the range 0.5 to 0.3 *pro rata*. For example, if HW Portsmouth is 4.2, the correction will be −0.4 m so HW Cowes will be 3.8 m.

Times
In a similar way, the times of high water and low water can be interpolated. From figure 1.6 it can be seen that when high water is at midnight or midday (GMT) at Portsmouth, high water at Cowes is 15 minutes earlier than Portsmouth, and when high water is at 0600 or 1800 GMT at Portsmouth, and when high water is at 0600 or

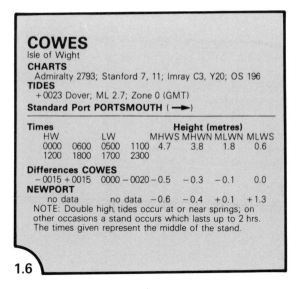

COWES
Isle of Wight
CHARTS
  Admiralty 2793; Stanford 7, 11; Imray C3, Y20; OS 196
TIDES
  +0023 Dover; ML 2.7; Zone 0 (GMT)
Standard Port PORTSMOUTH (→)

Times				Height (metres)			
HW		LW		MHWS	MHWN	MLWN	MLWS
0000	0600	0500	1100	4.7	3.8	1.8	0.6
1200	1800	1700	2300				

Differences COWES
−0015	+0015	0000	−0020	−0.5	−0.3	−0.1	0.0

NEWPORT
no data		no data	−0.6	−0.4	+0.1	+1.3

NOTE: Double high, tides occur at or near springs; on other occasions a stand occurs which lasts up to 2 hrs. The times given represent the middle of the stand.

1.6

1800 GMT at Portsmouth, the high water at Cowes is 15 minutes later. Thus there is a range of differences of up to 30 minutes (between − 15 minutes and + 15 minutes). The working is shown in example 4, and the results summarised in the table. Start by looking at the HW times in the two left-hand columns in figure 1.6 and choosing the pair that the HW time you wish to correct lies between (0000-0600, 0600-1200, 1200-1800, 1800-0000. Note that you can interpolate diagonally as well as across in this group of times). Round off the HW time you are correcting to the nearest half-hour when the range of differences is as small as this.

Example 4
(a) Find the time of HW Cowes for the following times of HW Portsmouth.
HW 0037
0037 = approx 1/12th the difference 0000 − 0600
From figure 1.6,
correction for 0000 = − 15 minutes
correction for 0600 = + 15 minutes
Therefore   range = 30 minutes
correction for 0037 = − 15 + (30 × 1/12)
$$= − 15 + 3$$
$$= − 12 \text{ minutes}$$
HW Cowes is HW Portsmouth minus 12 minutes

HW 1250
1200 = − 15 minutes
1800 = + 15 minutes
1250 = approx 1/6th difference 1200 – 1800
Correction for 1250 = −15 + (1/6 × 30)
$\qquad\qquad\qquad = − 15 + 5$
$\qquad\qquad\qquad = − 10$ minutes
HW Cowes is HW Portsmouth minus 10 minutes.

(b) Find the time of LW Cowes for the following times of LW Portsmouth.

LW 0547
Correction for 0500 = 0
Correction for 1100 = − 20 minutes
Difference = approx 1/6th of 20 minutes
$\qquad\qquad = 3$ minutes
LW Cowes is LW Portsmouth minus 3 minutes

LW 1810
Correction for 1700 = 0
Correction for 2300 = − 20 minutes
Difference = approx 1/6th of 20 minutes
$\qquad\qquad = 3$ minutes
LW Cowes is LW Portsmouth minus 3 minutes

These interpolations are summarised in the table.

The data shown in figure 1.6 is from the *Macmillan and Silk Cut Nautical Almanac* but it follows a standard pattern originally laid down by the *Admiralty Tide Tables*.

Conclusion

Tide tables will give the times of high and low water for standard and secondary ports, and hence the range, duration and the state of the tide with respect to springs and neaps. Using a chart in conjunction with the tide tables, you can predict the depth at any time, the rise of tide at any time, or the time at which a depth will be achieved. In order to predict tidal *stream* you need to use your tide tables in conjunction with a tidal atlas, or a chart with diamonds on it. This is covered in the next section.

Tidal atlases

These can be either general or local, and their function is to show the tidal streams for the areas they cover for each hour of the tidal cycle (related to a standard port). A tidal atlas is a vital tool of the trade and must be studied with care as part of your pre-race planning. You must know the times of the tide for the relevant standard port before you can use a tidal atlas. Figure 1.7 shows a typical page from a tidal atlas, and is for a time three hours after high water at Devonport.

In most areas around the world where tidal streams have an effect on yacht racing, some kind of tidal atlas is available. It may well be a national publication, such as the British and American tidal atlases (for example UK Tidal Atlas NP 337 – Solent and Adjacent Waters; NP 265 – France, West Coast, etc.) or the diagrams of tidal streams may appear in a local almanac. The format is nearly always the same: the reference is given to a standard port, and 13 small pictures of the area are shown, one for each hour of the tidal cycle. The tidal streams are shown by arrows, with the rates at springs and neaps alongside them.

Corrected tidal predictions for Cowes on 1 March

	HW (m)	Time (GMT)	LW (m)	Time (GMT)	HW (m)	Time (GMT)	LW (m)	Time (GMT)
Portsmouth	4.90	0037	0.50	0547	4.80	1250	0.40	1810
Corrections	−0.50	−12	0	−03	−0.50	−10	0	−03
Cowes	4.40	0025	0.50	0544	4.30	1240	0.40	1807

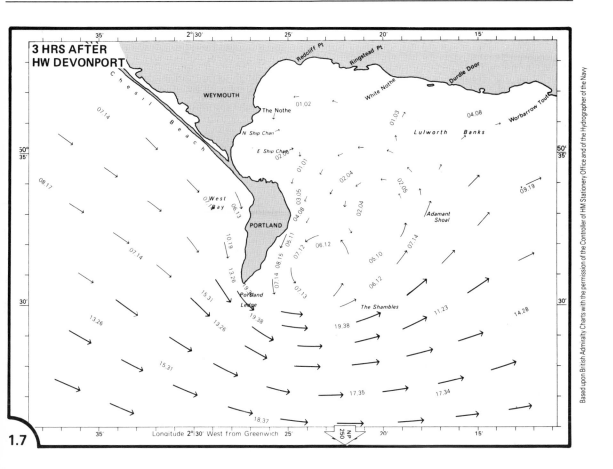

3 HRS AFTER HW DEVONPORT

1.7

Based upon British Admiralty Charts with the permission of the Controller of HM Stationery Office and of the Hydrographer of the Navy

Marking up your atlas

The first thing to do is to look up the time of high water at the standard port for the day of your race. Convert this to local time (i.e. add an hour for Summer Time if necessary). Next, write the time of high water on the picture showing high water/standard port, choosing a piece of land or some other part of the drawing where it won't cover up the tidal stream arrows. Now you can subtract one hour and write it on the previous picture (one hour before high water).

The process is repeated backwards and forwards until every picture has a time on it. This is a very important piece of pre-race planning, since it shows the tidal streams in each part of the race area for each hour.

Instructions for use

Each tidal atlas will contain instructions for its use in the front. Broadly, though, these are common sense and run as follows:

- The direction of the tidal streams are shown by arrows.
- Usually the arrows are heavier where the tidal streams are stronger.
- Figures against the arrows usually give the mean neap and spring rates in tenths of a knot. Thus 19,34 indicates a mean neap rate of 1.9 knots and a mean spring rate of 3.4 knots. The comma between the two rates indicates the approximate position at which the observations were obtained. Bear in mind that these are small-scale charts, so it is quite

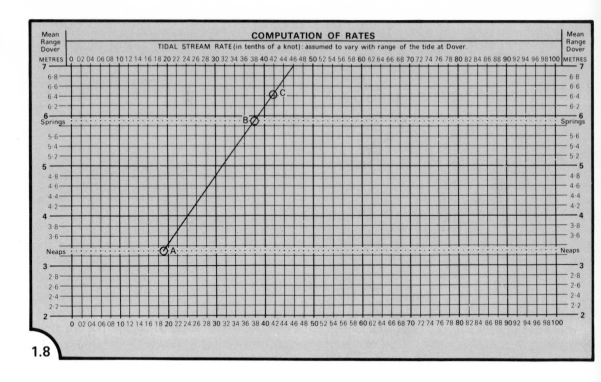

COMPUTATION OF RATES

TIDAL STREAM RATE (in tenths of a knot): assumed to vary with range of the tide at Dover.

1.8

Tidal Streams referred to HW at DEVONPORT

HW 1540

	Hours	Ⓐ 50°29·5N 2 35·1W			Ⓑ 50°36·3N 2 34·8W			Ⓒ 50°28·0N 2 31·4W			Ⓓ 50°30·3N 2 29·2W			Ⓔ 50°33·3N 2 29·2W			Ⓕ 50°29·6N 2 26·6W			Ⓖ 50°26·3N 2 26·4W			Ⓗ 50°34·2N 2 21·9W			Ⓘ 50°30·9N 2 20·0W			Ⓙ 50°27·2N 2 16·8W			Hours
		Dir	Sp	Np	Dir	Sp	Np	Dir	Sp	Np	Dir	Sp	Np	Dir	Sp	Np	Dir	Sp	Np	Dir	Sp	Np	Dir	Sp	Np	Dir	Sp	Np	Dir	Sp	Np	
0940	6	286	1·6	0·8	290	0·9	0·4	264	2·0	1·0	347	2·4	1·2	305	0·6	0·3	249	7·0	3·5	263	1·5	0·7	232	1·6	0·8	245	1·6	0·8	260	1·7	0·8	6
1040	5	290	2·8	1·4	299	1·5	0·7	282	3·2	1·6	333	2·2	1·1	335	0·8	0·4	240	7·0	3·5	270	2·8	1·4	231	1·4	0·7	246	2·3	1·1	257	3·2	1·6	5
1140	4	302	3·2	1·6	302	1·4	0·7	289	3·8	1·9	275	1·5	0·8	012	0·7	0·3	236	6·4	3·2	267	3·6	1·8	230	1·2	0·6	246	2·4	1·2	256	3·5	1·7	4
1240	3	318	2·9	1·5	325	0·7	0·3	283	3·4	1·7	226	2·1	1·0	127	1·3	0·7	228	4·8	2·4	261	3·0	1·5	239	0·9	0·4	249	1·8	0·9	252	2·8	1·4	3
1340	2	323	1·7	0·9	045	0·5	0·2	280	2·3	1·1	192	2·6	1·3	133	1·8	0·8	219	2·0	1·0	258	1·5	0·7	332	0·3	0·1	259	0·8	0·4	258	1·5	0·8	2
1440	1	000	1·0	0·5	104	0·6	0·3	280	1·0	0·5	162	3·2	1·6	134	2·2	1·1	112	0·9	0·5	158	0·2	0·1	048	0·8	0·4	048	0·6	0·3	350	0·1	0·1	1
1540	HW	080	1·3	0·6	129	1·0	0·5	083	0·8	0·4	136	4·0	2·0	143	2·0	1·0	111	4·5	2·2	105	1·6	0·8	034	0·8	0·4	051	1·8	0·9	079	1·9	0·9	HW
1640	1	100	2·4	1·2	127	1·3	0·6	097	2·5	1·2	136	3·8	1·9	141	1·7	0·8	102	5·6	2·8	101	2·8	1·4	030	0·7	0·3	043	2·5	1·2	082	3·5	1·7	1
1740	2	111	2·5	1·3	127	1·5	0·7	099	3·2	1·6	142	3·5	1·7	145	1·5	0·8	109	4·6	2·3	101	3·6	1·8	344	0·3	0·2	050	1·9	1·0	081	4·0	2·0	2
1840	3	124	2·6	1·3	131	1·4	0·7	101	3·1	1·5	144	3·1	1·5	146	1·4	0·7	119	3·8	1·9	108	3·7	1·8	231	0·4	0·2	058	1·2	0·6	078	3·4	1·7	3
1940	4	126	1·9	1·0	139	1·0	0·5	107	2·2	1·1	157	1·9	0·9	156	1·0	0·5	138	2·7	1·3	117	2·2	1·1	224	0·9	0·5	066	0·6	0·3	075	2·5	1·2	4
2040	5	148	0·6	0·3	158	0·3	0·1	113	0·8	0·4	208	0·8	0·4	176	0·4	0·2	209	2·2	1·1	121	0·7	0·3	231	1·5	0·7	066	0·6	0·3	350	0·1	0·1	5
2140	6	283	1·1	0·5	289	0·6	0·3	255	1·5	0·7	345	1·7	0·8	300	0·5	0·2	247	5·2	2·6	261	1·0	0·5	230	1·6	0·8	237	1·4	0·7	260	1·0	0·5	6

(Rows 0940–1440: Before HW; 1640–2140: After HW)

	Hours	Ⓚ 50°29·8N 2 12·6W			Ⓛ 50°36·3N 2 12·6W			Ⓜ 50°33·7N 2 00·0W			Ⓝ 50°28·3N 1 59·7W			Ⓞ 50°37·0N 1 51·0W			Ⓟ 50°27·5N 1 47·0W			Ⓠ 50°33·8N 1 45·9W			Ⓡ 50°35·5N 1 38·5W			Ⓢ 50°42·9N 1 38·5W			Ⓣ 50°39·7N 1 37·2W			Hours
		Dir	Sp	Np	Dir	Sp	Np	Dir	Sp	Np	Dir	Sp	Np	Dir	Sp	Np	Dir	Sp	Np	Dir	Sp	Np	Dir	Sp	Np	Dir	Sp	Np	Dir	Sp	Np	
0940	6	277	1·8	0·9	277	1·9	1·0	257	1·6	0·8	261	1·2	0·6	241	1·5	0·7	263	2·0	1·0	256	1·4	0·7	264	1·3	0·7	281	0·9	0·5	277	2·0	1·1	6
1040	5	272	2·3	1·1	280	2·3	1·1	256	2·6	1·3	258	2·5	1·2	236	2·4	1·2	263	2·9	1·4	260	2·2	1·1	266	2·0	1·1	276	1·0	0·5	264	2·3	1·5	5
1140	4	272	3·5	1·7	278	2·3	1·1	258	3·1	1·5	252	3·4	1·7	231	2·3	1·1	266	2·9	1·4	249	2·7	1·3	265	2·2	1·3	266	0·9	0·4	254	2·9	1·6	4
1240	3	276	2·8	1·4	279	1·7	0·8	257	2·4	1·2	252	3·0	1·5	234	1·8	0·9	266	2·2	1·1	252	2·1	1·0	265	1·8	1·0	260	0·7	0·3	254	2·8	1·4	3
1340	2	288	1·8	0·9	296	0·6	0·3	259	1·6	0·8	250	1·8	0·9	227	1·0	0·5	275	1·3	0·6	246	1·1	0·6	267	1·0	0·6	260	0·2	0·1	270	0·9	0·5	2
1440	1	355	0·5	0·3	063	0·8	0·4	102	0·4	0·2	296	0·5	0·3	048	0·2	0·1	014	0·4	0·2	150	0·2	0·1	350	0·2	0·1	081	0·5	0·3	054	0·8	0·5	1
1540	HW	056	1·4	0·7	081	1·9	0·9	069	1·7	0·8	057	1·0	0·5	052	1·2	0·6	075	1·3	0·6	094	1·0	0·5	076	0·9	0·5	093	0·8	0·4	077	1·9	1·1	HW
1640	1	068	2·6	1·3	083	2·2	1·1	068	2·7	1·3	074	2·1	1·0	052	1·9	0·9	089	2·4	1·2	075	2·0	1·0	084	1·5	0·8	100	1·0	0·5	088	2·6	1·5	1
1740	2	071	3·0	1·5	077	2·2	1·1	075	2·6	1·3	078	2·9	1·4	057	2·1	1·1	088	2·9	1·4	075	2·3	1·1	087	2·0	1·1	092	0·9	0·4	087	2·6	1·5	2
1840	3	067	2·6	1·3	070	1·9	0·9	079	2·2	1·1	074	2·8	1·4	055	2·0	1·0	085	2·5	1·2	075	2·0	1·0	089	2·0	1·1	088	0·7	0·4	087	2·2	1·2	3
1940	4	062	1·8	0·9	055	1·0	0·5	079	1·5	0·7	081	2·0	1·0	046	1·3	0·7	085	1·6	0·8	070	1·2	0·6	091	1·4	0·8	088	0·2	0·1	087	2·1	1·2	4
2040	5	048	0·5	0·2	310	0·5	0·3	076	0·5	0·3	074	0·7	0·3	103	0·3	0·2	065	0·5	0·2	109	0·4	0·2	098	0·6	0·3	260	0·3	0·1	350	0·4	0·2	5
2140	6	279	1·2	0·6	280	1·4	0·7	251	1·0	0·5	283	0·6	0·3	242	1·1	0·6	258	1·4	0·7	254	1·0	0·5	257	0·7	0·4	275	0·5	0·3	282	1·6	0·9	6

1.9

important to remember where that comma is because several degrees of interpolation are required. These are as follows.

Interpolation

You have to interpolate between springs and neaps, so use your judgement of whether the tide is quarter springs, half springs, etc. Alternatively, you can work this out more accurately using a 'computation of rates' grid (often to be found in the front of the tidal stream atlas). This is based on the mean range of the day, the idea being that a large range will give a large tidal stream while a small range gives a small tidal stream.

Example 5

What is the tidal stream at Portland Ledge three hours after HW Devonport, on a day when the range is 6.4 metres?
From the tidal atlas (figure 1.7) the tide speeds are found to be 19,38 (1.9 knots neaps, 3.8 knots springs).
    Plot points A (neaps) and B (springs) on the 'computation of rates' grid in figure 1.8.
    Join A to B with a straight line, extended if necessary.
    Read off the tidal stream for today's range (point C).
The tidal stream is 4.2 knots.

If the time you are interested in falls between two pictures, interpolation between the hours must be made. Look at the two hourly pictures which bracket the time in question (say the start time of a race) and try to form some kind of mental picture about what the tide will be doing in the intervening 60 minutes. Usually, unless the tide is on the turn (from flood to ebb or vice versa), it is sufficient just to interpolate the rates. If the tide is on the turn, then decide whether the turn comes nearer the second hour than the first, and assume slack water at about (say) 40 minutes past the first hour.
    Interpolation is also required between arrows. These are small-scale charts, and the exact position of the start may well be between two arrows. Remember the comma between the speeds is the position at which the observation was taken; try to draw pencil lines parallel to the run of the tide between arrows or commas, and then make an estimate as to the actual tide running in the position of the start. It is not a bad idea to sketch these lines on a separate sheet of paper if you are dealing with a critical decision.

Chart diamonds

If a tidal atlas is available then this is your most useful source of information. Otherwise (and particularly for offshore work) chart diamonds give a wealth of tidal data.
    A chart diamond (or a tidal diamond) is simply a small magenta diamond on the chart with a letter in it. In one of the corners of the chart, away from congestion and possibly on a land mass, is a set of tables. An example of a typical set of tables from the Channel chart is given in figure 1.9.
    The table shows the spring and neap rates and directions. Note that these are the directions in which the tide will flow (e.g. 90 degrees means that the tide will flow to the east). Note also that they are true directions; to convert tidal bearings to compass bearings you need to apply the local magnetic variation (given on the chart near the compass rose).
    To use the tidal diamonds:
1 Pencil in the time of HW for the standard port (in this case 1540 at Devonport).
2 Pencil in, at the side of the table, the times for the six hours before and the six hours after HW, so that the rate and direction of the tide at the position of the diamond can be ascertained every hour (see figure 1.9).
3 Refer to the actual diamonds on the chart nearest the course, and note the tidal streams.
    You will need to interpolate between springs and neaps, between the positions of adjacent diamonds, and for times between the hourly pieces of data.
    In fact, the information given in a tidal atlas is the same as that given by the diamonds: if you had 13 charts and drew up the pattern of tides on each based on tidal diamond information, you would have created a tidal atlas.

2 Local effects

In your pre-race preparation you should by now have a chart of the area in which the race is to take place, with the predicted times of high water and low water marked upon it, and you should also have marked up your relevant tidal diamonds with the expected currents on the chart (or at least have marked the time of high water for the standard port over the table of tidal rates – see figure 1.9 on page 16). If you have a tidal atlas, this should be marked up with the times of the day during which the race will be held, so that you can turn to the hourly page as the race progresses to discover what is happening to the tidal streams. In other words you are armed with the knowledge of predicted depths and predicted tidal streams.

However, this is not all you need to know. There are such things as 'local effects' which will modify the predictions. Briefly, these can be split into two headings:

- Weather effects.
- The effects of geography or topography – land masses, rivers, shallow patches, etc.

Weather effects

A wind that has been blowing for some time over open water will set up a current in line with the direction of the wind. At first this will only affect the surface water (especially if it is fairly fresh and/or warm), but because of friction, the depth at which this current is felt increases. David Houghton, in his book *Wind Strategy* in this series, has described how a wind of 10 knots blowing over a surface layer of warm water about one metre deep will accelerate it to a speed of a knot or more after 10 hours of blowing. This was measured at Acapulco in the 1968 Olympics.

David Houghton also indicates that in higher latitudes a marked swing in direction will be observed due to the rotation of the earth, although the initial current direction will be dead downwind. The swing is to the right in the northern hemisphere and to the left in the southern hemisphere, and can be up to 80 degrees off the wind line after a prolonged period of constant wind.

It is always good practice to observe the start mark buoys and committee boat to discover the true surface current at the start, in spite of all the theoretical work put in beforehand.

Some examples of wind effects

In the English Channel when the wind blows from a westerly direction for a prolonged period, the ebb tides (flowing to the west) get later and later (and smaller and smaller). When the wind ceases (or after a depression has crossed the area and a west wind turns into an east wind) the next ebb tidal stream is usually about 20 per cent more than its predicted value in rate, although its direction remains relatively constant.

In the Baltic, after a prolonged period of southerly winds when the water is piled up in the northern part of the sea and the Gulf of Finland, a southerly current of up to seven knots is created as soon as the wind stops blowing and the water runs south. Similar effects are noted in Long Island Sound, in certain areas of the Mediterranean, as well as in many other places.

Summary

Remember that if a strong wind has been blowing for a prolonged period over a constricted or channelled patch of water it is likely to have the following effects.

- The wind creates a downwind current, which swings due to the earth's movement after the wind has been blowing for some time.
- It forces the tidal stream flowing contra to the wind to be late and reduced in strength.
- When the wind stops blowing, the water will regain equilibrium by flowing much harder (and for slightly longer) in the direction from which the wind was blowing. This effect ceases after about 24 to 36 hours, and is strongest in the first 12 hours.

An example of the latter effect occurred in the Channel race in the Admiral's Cup series a few years ago. I was navigating the yacht 'Yeoman XX' which was a member of the British team, and we rounded CH1 Buoy off Cherbourg in a good position, bound for the Nab Tower to be rounded to port and then on to the finish in the Solent. The lay line was 032 degrees, and a small depression centred in northern France was moving east rather quickly, which gave initially at least ENE winds. Knowing the flood tide would carry us past the Nab (to be rounded to port) at the end of the passage, we sailed free and fast. As expected, the wind headed as the depression carried on eastwards (see figure 2.1). When St.Catherine's Light was sighted the following morning, we were heading in towards Bembridge Ledge, close-hauled on the starboard tack, having hardened up to 037 degrees, and the wind having backed to NE x E. In spite of the predicted tidal stream which should have carried us upstream and past the Nab, the tidal assistance expected did not materialise due to the prolonged easterly wind, and we were forced to put in four tacks to round the Nab, thus losing several places to other boats which had held up to the east.

The moral of this is always to hold up for a mark if there is any danger of a predicted tide being held back by wind. It is faster to free off at the end of a leg than to have to tack.

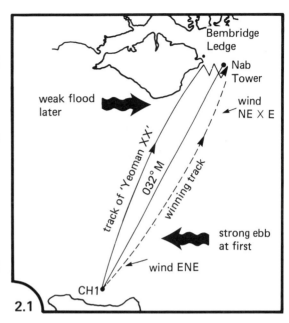

2.1

Geography and topography

Shallow water effects

It ought to be engraved upon every helmsman's heart that the tidal stream is less inshore than offshore. This is due to the friction of the bottom of the sea. It is very important when racing against the prevailing water flow to get close inshore so that the adverse current is thereby less. With a rocky, abruptly rising coast, it is necessary to get very close indeed (ten or fifteen metres from the shore if possible) to avoid tidal flow.

A good example of this is Portland Bill in a flood tide, where the large basalt chunks break the tide up within a metre or two from the shore, when it is running at perhaps 2 or 3 knots ten metres further off. Many a Fastnet race has been won by boats bumping from outcrop to outcrop to cheat the flood tide.

Turn of the tide

When sailing on the turn of the tide, remember that the tidal stream turns inshore first.
Adverse tide before the turn. If you are sailing against the tidal stream, it is important to get inshore to catch the early tidal stream there and get a favourable push while boats still out in the main stream will continue to be retarded.
Favourable tide before the turn. What is not so generally realised is that the last of a favourable tidal stream will give a substantial advantage to a boat that stays out in it. There always seems to be a rush to get inshore regardless, but since the tide turns first inshore (see figure 2.2) boats inshore will stem the first of the adverse tidal stream, while a boat remaining offshore will enjoy favourable tidal stream for perhaps twenty minutes or half an hour longer. Of course, time has to be allowed to get inshore to reduce the adverse effect when the tide does turn offshore.

It follows from this that there is a time – at the turn of the tide – when the tidal stream is *stronger* inshore than offshore because it turns there first. After the first hour or so this position is reversed and there is a constant flow with the inshore flow again being less than the offshore flow.

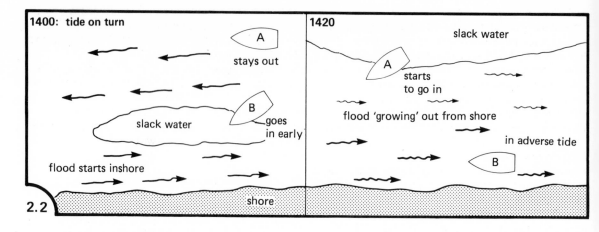

2.2

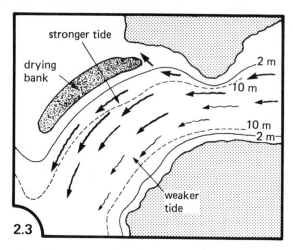

2.3

Tide in a curved channel

Usually where tide is flowing in a channel it is strongest in the middle of the deepwater channel and weakest in the shallows at the sides, due to friction at the bottom. However, sometimes a channel or estuary has a bend or a long shoal which causes the current to curve due to a 'piling up' effect. In this case it is stronger on the outer curve of the bend (towards the entrance in figure 2.3).

Shoals

Because of the effects of bottom friction, most tidal streams and currents are slower over shoals. If the tidal stream is against a boat then its effect can be reduced by sailing in shallow water.

With an outlying bar strong tides flow over that bar because the water flow is constricted. A good

example of this is the Shingles Bank, off the Needles in the Isle of Wight, where the maximum tide is found between the Port Hand Buoys and the Shingles Bank, and not in the main shipping channel.

Eddies

In bays there are usually substantial eddies where a strong tidal stream persists. This can be judged from an inspection of the tidal atlas, but it really requires a certain amount of local knowledge, as well as judgement. It is well worth watching local sailors to verify the point.

Behind every island, or in a bay behind a peninsula, there will be a whirlpool and a counter-current close to the shore. Many examples can be found; a good illustration is that on the English coast, on the eastern side of Portland Bill. Reference to figure 1.7 in the last chapter will indicate that with a strong flood tide going up the Channel and reaching nearly 4 knots on spring tides, at a time three hours after HW Devonport, not only is there a whirlpool on the eastern side of Portland Bill but a strong counter-current going westward exists between three and five miles north of the Shambles Bank, and an inshore current going SSW exists along the edge of Portland Bill.

It is also worth noting from figure 1.7 what a large tidal stream there is out in the Channel and how very little tidal stream exists inshore around Weymouth Bay and the Lulworth Banks. Marked differences in tidal stream of this nature are very important in races held in this area.

Eddies, whirlpools and counter-currents are very sharply defined and a difference of as little as 30 metres between two boats can mean a difference of 3 or 4 knots in their speed over the ground for this reason. It is important to be bold and get very close in as indicated above. Sometimes a distinct 'tide line' appears on the water, marking the edge of the current. Watch for this and get on the right side of the line!

Tide rips and overfalls

Where a line of rock juts out from the shore and continues on under the sea at a level significantly above the ocean floor, overfalls, tide rips and races will be created where the tidal stream sweeps across this line of rock. Again, the race off Portland Bill, as well as the overfalls off Anvil Point and St Alban's Head, are typical examples. These are predictable effects, and warnings about them are marked on the chart. In heavy weather with spring tides, the race off Portland Bill can be positively dangerous. In general tidal streams are slowed by underwater obstructions, because much of the energy contained is used in the rips, standing waves and races, and not in tidal movement. This is the extreme manifestation of the effect of friction.

The type of sea produced by these upwellings, races and similar effects makes competitive sailing very difficult. For this reason, areas known to be prone to these effects should be avoided during a race, and the standard method of avoidance is either to go offshore (if the tide is with you) or very close inshore (if the tide is against you).

Rivers

Rivers have two effects on water flow. Near the river mouth there will be superimposed on the tidal stream a current which is due to the outflow from the river. This is predictable and local in its effect.

River water is generally at a different temperature from the sea into which it is flowing. If it is colder than the sea it will sink rapidly, and the only effect on current will be local. However, if the river water is significantly warmer than the sea water (this can be expected in tropical areas, whereas in more temperate climes the sea is likely to be warmer than the rivers) the river water will stay on top of the sea water and influence tidal streams for a significant distance. Quoting David Houghton again, a river outflow some 80 kilometres down the coast from the sailing area at Acapulco, Mexico, caused what was known as a 'slippery sea', which was a top layer of warm fresh water, very prone to wind influence and behaving entirely differently from the movement of the colder, heavier sea water.

Before the race

On a short, inshore race, or in an area where an Olympic course is to be laid, it is possible to check the prevailing water flow by going out the evening before the race (or early on the morning of the race) and observing the current at strategic points on the proposed course. This can be done in one of two ways – either the boat can be anchored or tied up to a buoy and objects dropped over the side to observe the rate and direction of drift; or small dan buoys can be dropped over the side to anchor themselves on the bottom and the rate and direction of drift can be observed from the boat by comparing its position with the dan buoy. Convenient equipment for this exercise is a number of plastic bottles with fishing line wrapped around them and a lead sinker on the other end. These can be easily retrieved and are cheap to produce. Some ocean-racing yachts carry this equipment to drop (out of sight of land) to check the tide, although with the advent of electronics in racing, there are now better ways to do this.

Conclusion

I hope I have illustrated how important it is to calculate properly the predicted tides and tidal streams. Before the race local effects must be estimated and taken into account. Every effort should be made to compare what is actually happening with what is predicted. It is likely that if you go through this whole exercise, you will know more about water flow in the area of the course than anybody else. The next chapters are designed to assist you in using this information to your best advantage.

3   Basic tidal tactics

In the first two chapters we looked at how to predict tides, and their magnitude in any locality, and how the local effects of geographic factors or persistent winds can modify the predictions published in almanacs. It is now time to examine the basic principles of tidal tactics. In later chapters we will put these principles to use in actual race situations.

The wind perceived on a boat is affected by three separate factors. The first is the true wind experienced at that place, irrespective of boat movement. The second is the wind generated by the passage of the boat through the air, which is in an opposite direction to the boat's course and at the same speed. These two are combined to form a resultant which is usually known as the *apparent wind*. However, when the motion of the boat over the sea is modified by a tidal current, the apparent wind perceived aboard will be the resultant of waterflow, boat motion through the water and true wind. These three factors

contributing to the apparent wind are usually represented by the *vector system*. Let's see first how the vector system works when there is no water movement.

Apparent wind with no water flow

If you are sailing in still water (i.e. with no water flow at all) you will perceive an apparent wind, which is the resultant of the *motion wind* (blowing in the opposite direction to your course and at the same speed as the boat) and the *true wind*.

This can be illustrated by drawing arrows to represent the wind on a vector diagram. Each arrow should be in the same direction as the wind it represents, and the length of each arrow shows the speed of the wind (see figure 3.1). These arrows can be considered as two sides of a triangle: draw in the third side and you have the resultant of the two winds – the apparent wind. You can now see that when a boat is beating the apparent

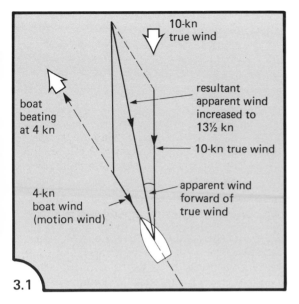

3.1

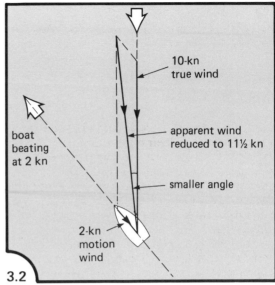

3.2

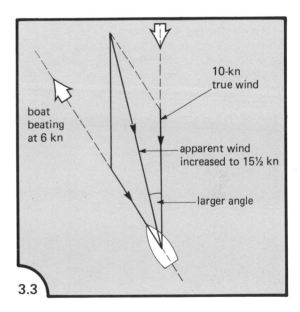

3.3

wind comes forward of the true wind and increases in velocity.

In figures 3.2 and 3.3 I have varied the speed of the boat, while the true wind remains the same. In figure 3.2 boat speed has been reduced to 2 knots, and you can see that as the speed reduces the apparent wind gets nearer to the true wind both in velocity and angle. In figure 3.3 the speed of the boat has increased to 6 knots. In this case the apparent wind moves further forward and increases in velocity.

To sum up: when a boat is beating, an *increase* in boat speed results in the wind coming forward (heading) and a *decrease* in boat speed results in the wind coming from further aft (freeing). An increase in boat speed results in an increase in apparent wind, and a decrease in boat speed results in the wind reducing.

If a boat is beating up to the windward mark the heading and freeing effects, as well as the change in velocities mentioned above, will affect the course the boat steers and the speed at which it travels.

A boat stopped in the water will only experience the true wind. At the other extreme a motor boat going at 10 knots in a flat calm with no tidal stream will experience a 10-knot wind directly on the bow caused by its own motion.

The effect of waterflow on boats beating

It should be stated clearly here that tide has two effects on boats racing. The first effect is on the apparent wind strength and direction. The second effect is the movement of the boat downtide, caused by the velocity of the water flowing over the sea bed. We are only concerned with the first

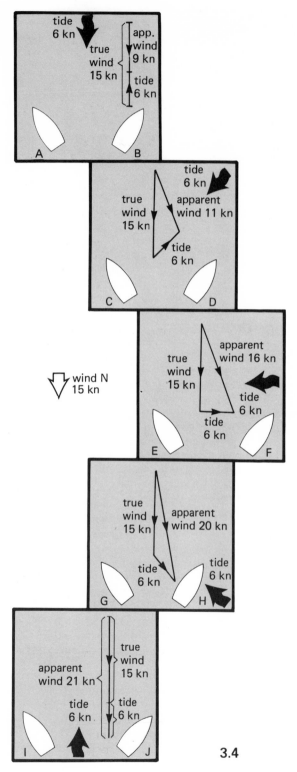

effect for the moment – the effect on the apparent (perceived) wind.

A tidal stream has two effects on apparent wind. It changes the *direction* of the apparent wind, and it changes the *velocity* of the apparent wind.

Figure 3.4 shows a constant true wind coming from the top of the page (north) at a velocity of 15 knots, and a tidal stream with a velocity of 6 knots flowing at varying angles to the two boats which are beating up to the top of the page. Small vector diagrams show the effect of the tide on the true wind to give the apparent wind.

In the top picture the tidal stream is with the wind. This displaces both boats A and B bodily away from the wind and therefore reduces the apparent wind, so that the apparent wind equals the true wind (15 knots) minus the tidal velocity (6 knots), giving 9 knots over the deck. If the tidal stream is in line with the true wind then no change in direction of the apparent wind results.

In the next picture down boats C and D are beating with the tide at 225 degrees (i.e. at 45 degrees to the true wind). As shown in the small vector diagram the effect of this is that the apparent wind backs away from the true wind and lessens in velocity. Boat D is thereby lifted towards the mark at the top of the page and boat C is headed.

In the next picture the tide flows in a direction of 270 degrees which is at 90 degrees to the true wind. The effect is similar to that of the previous figure except that the angular displacement (backing) of the true wind is at its maximum. Boat F is very much lifted whereas boat E is very much headed.

Boats G and H experience a similar effect with the tide displaced a further 45 degrees and flowing in the direction of 315 degrees. However, since the tide is now against the true wind both boats are being pushed into the true wind and the perceived velocity over their decks is increased. Nonetheless boat H is lifted and boat G is headed, although not so much as in the previous example. Both boats can be expected to increase their speed because of the increased wind.

Finally, with the tidal stream in the reciprocal direction to the true wind, there is again no change in the apparent wind's angle. Both boats I and J are being pushed into the wind by the tide which is going north (360 degrees) and the apparent

3.4

wind is increased but not changed in direction. Both boats will be going somewhat faster due to the increased apparent wind (this is in addition to the fact that they are approaching the mark rather more quickly because the tide is carrying them towards it).

From this a few rules can be formulated.

Wind strength

- If the tidal stream is *opposing* the apparent wind, the apparent wind will *increase* in velocity (boats I and J).
- If the tidal stream is *going with* the apparent wind, the apparent wind will *reduce* in velocity (boats A and B).
- If the tidal stream is at *right angles* to the apparent wind, the velocity of the apparent wind will not be much affected (boats E and F).

Wind direction

- If the tidal stream sets towards the *left* of the apparent wind, boats on the starboard tack will be headed and boats on the port tack will be freed.

- If the tidal stream sets towards the *right* of the apparent wind, boats on the starboard tack will be freed and boats on the port tack will be headed (this is the mirror image of figure 3.4).

The effect of waterflow on boats running and reaching

Figure 3.5 shows four examples of the effect of tidal stream on boats running or reaching. In the top square, boat A is reaching and boat B is running. Since the tidal stream is in line with the true wind blowing from the north (top of the page) the effect is as before, to push both boats away from the wind and thereby reduce the strength of the true wind by the speed of the tidal stream. If the tide is running at 6 knots and the true wind is at 15 knots this will modify the wind on both boats to a velocity of 9 knots (i.e. the difference between the two) with no change in direction.

The lower square shows boat F running and boat E reaching. In this case the tide, though still in line with the true wind, is pushing directly

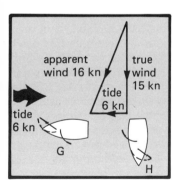

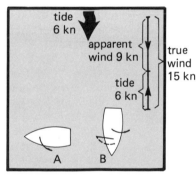

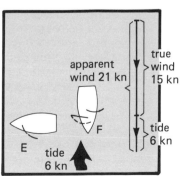

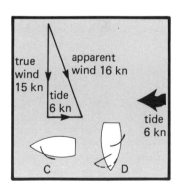

3.5

against it. Again, there is no change in wind direction since both forces are in line. Since both boats are being pushed towards the wind, the apparent wind is increased – it is the sum of the true wind and the tidal stream effect (in this case 21 knots).

Boat C (right-hand square) is reaching with the tide behind it, going in a direction of 270 degrees. The effect of this with a northerly true wind of 15 knots is shown in the small vector diagram. Boat C is headed because its actual speed over the ground is increased by the tide behind it. This brings the apparent wind forward of the beam and increases it in velocity. Boat D, which is running, will find that the wind appears to back and the sails will have to be sheeted in slightly as the wind comes around from dead astern on to the starboard quarter. This is important, since if boat D had just rounded a mark she could go off on either gybe were the true wind only to be considered. Taking the tide into consideration, it is obvious that the run will have to be set up with a starboard spinnaker pole since the wind will be on the starboard quarter.

Finally, in the left-hand square, boat G is running with the tide on the bow. Because the boat is thereby slowed up by 6 knots the apparent wind moves aft (veers). This is the opposite situation to boat C in the previous example. Boat G may now set a spinnaker whereas with the true wind alone this might not have been possible. Boat H is running; this time, due to the tidal stream being in the opposite direction to the previous example (with boat D), the wind will come around from dead astern to the port quarter. Were boat H to have just rounded a mark it would have been necessary to have set up a port spinnaker pole. Appreciation of the tidal effect on the apparent wind is vital when planning the strategy for the next leg.

A few rules can be formulated for reaching and running.

- When the tide is *with* the wind, the direction of the apparent wind remains the same but its strength is lessened.
- When the tide is *against* the wind, the wind's direction remains the same but its strength is increased.
- When the tide is in the *same* direction as the boat's progress, the apparent wind comes ahead.

- When the tide is *against* the boat's progress, the apparent wind comes astern.

The effect of tidal stream on position

In inshore racing, when it is necessary to travel from mark to mark in a relatively short period, deviations in position due to the tide must be corrected by steering a course which compensates for tidal drift. (This is *not* true in all cases in offshore races, as will be described later.)

In figure 3.6 the boat is travelling from mark A to mark C, a distance of 6½ miles due west. However, a current setting 145 degrees by 2 knots will put the boat in position B. The boat has been set 17 degrees to the south (i.e. has made good a course of 253 degrees) and has been slowed by about 1 knot (i.e. position B is about 5½ miles from position A). This is a fairly standard current triangle.

The method of calculating the offset of the current is shown in figure 3.7. Draw in the current as a line from mark A in the direction from which it will set (145 degrees) to a length which represents 1 hour of current (2 miles in this case). This gives you point D. Using compasses with a radius set to represent the boat's speed per hour (6½ miles), draw an arc to intersect the original course between marks A and C. This gives point E.

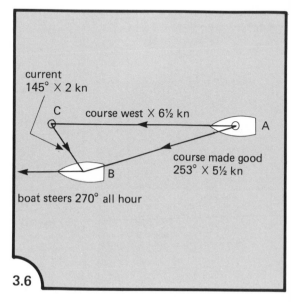

current
145° X 2 kn

C   course west X 6½ kn   A

course made good
253° X 5½ kn

B

boat steers 270° all hour

3.6

A line drawn between D and E gives the course to steer (285 degrees); the boat will 'crab' along the line A-C, pointing parallel with D-E. Its speed made good will be 5 knots (A-E in 1 hour) and it will take 1 hr 20 min to reach C (6½ miles divided by 5 knots). This is the standard vector diagram for the correction of course due to tidal stream or current.

Young's course corrector. A very handy instrument, for sale in most marine chandleries, is Captain Young's Course Corrector. This is a plastic gadget which reproduces the vector diagram in a reversed form, to correct for current. The course is dialled on the disc at the bottom of the instrument. The boat's speed is set against the direction and speed of current on the disc. At the top of the quadrant can be read off the degrees to add or subtract from the course to correct for current. The speed made good over the ground is shown in the centre slideway. You can carry this in your pocket, and with a knowledge of the direction and set of current, as well as the compass course between two marks and the approximate speed of the boat on the next leg, you can correct your course to allow for tidal stream.

Computers. Yacht racers have the advantage over dinghy sailors in that a lot of very clever people have gone to great lengths to programme tide, true wind, boat velocity, etc. into computers such as those made by Apple or Commodore. Instruments (Hercules, Rochester, etc.) exist to convert apparent wind readings into true wind (or at least wind over water). This has made gadgets like Young's Course Corrector obsolete on bigger boats, although there is some comfort in simplicity, and given the right information, the Course Corrector not only provides the right answers but also illustrates the triangles of forces in the correct orientation for the thinking tactician.

Tidal streams and light winds

We have looked at the effect of tide on the apparent wind given a constant true wind and a steady boat speed. The effect is enormously enhanced if strong tides combine with light true winds. This effect is twofold: firstly, the wind created by the tide (in the reciprocal direction) will be a much larger proportion of the apparent wind in these conditions. Secondly, the lighter the true wind is the slower the boat will go – this means that it will be longer exposed to tidal influence and will therefore be taken further off course.

It is especially important therefore in conditions of light winds and strong tides to take the following actions before starting the next leg of a race.
- Work out the tidally corrected course between the next two marks, so the helmsman can steer the correct course.
- Estimate the likely apparent wind (from boat speed, true wind and waterflow, using a vector diagram), so the sails can be set up correctly for the next leg.

Tidal gradient

So far we have been considering a constant tidal stream or waterflow. However, in the real world, tidal streams and currents vary across a stretch of water. These variations may well be caused by time (when the tide turns) or by geographical features (as described in Chapter 2). You should be aware of the likelihood of these tidal stream changes and be able to use them to your advantage.

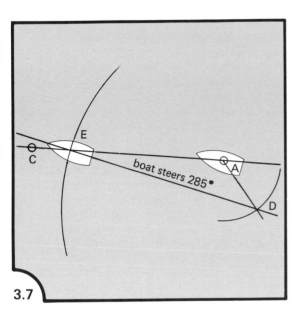

3.7

boat steers 285°

Example

One of the best examples of tidal gradient is a course going across the mouth of a bay. The windward leg offers the choice of either sailing out to sea or sailing into the bay. After a lot of effort I managed to draw a diagram showing this situation (figure 3.8) which combines most of the effects mentioned, including shallow water effects. This illustrates just how important tidal streams are in the scheme of things in a real race. Figure 3.8 at first sight appears alarmingly complex, but it will become clear as you read the step-by-step explanation (below) of the action as it unfolds. It is most important that you follow this through with care, because all the theoretical information given above has to be put together on the day of the race.

Putting it all together

Careful reference should be made to figure 3.8 while reading this section. The setting is a bay with gradients of tide which decrease and alter in direction in a typical fashion. At the mouth of the bay the tide runs strongly from headland to headland. As the inner shoreline of the bay is approached the tide follows more and more nearly the contour of the land, and becomes weaker through friction and the other local effects described.

An Olympic course (or at least one leg of it) is laid with the leeward mark on the south-western edge of the bay, and the weather mark near the north-eastern headland. The marks are 4 miles apart and lie in line with the true wind, which is blowing from the north-east at 10 knots. The wind is constant throughout the whole bay. The two course marks, as well as the tidal contours, are marked on the diagram.

Two boats are racing, A and B. Both have a speed through the water of 5 knots when tacking up to the weather mark, which is generated by a combination of the true wind speed of 10 knots and the boat-generated wind of 5 knots on the bow. If the apparent wind thus created is reduced, the boat speed will be reduced. Each boat sails 40 degrees off the true wind in absence of current. The incidence of current will alter this angle in each case.

Boats A and B start simultaneously from the leeward mark. Boat A takes off on starboard tack out to sea. A small wind diagram, including tide, boat speed and true wind, is given in the figure, and shows that the tide pushing on boat A's starboard beam (away from the wind) at 2 to 2½ knots means that the wind she experiences (tide-corrected apparent wind) is slightly reduced and heads the boat by 8 degrees. The actual line the boat takes is 48 degrees from the true wind.

The tide is also pushing the boat A away from the mark at a rate of 2 to 2½ knots, and when boat A tacks after 30 minutes, she has been pushed significantly further from the mark by the tide (about 1¼ miles as shown).

Boat B sets off on port tack. The tide here is less (about 1¼ knots) and almost directly on the bow. This reduces the boat's speed, and so the apparent wind is reduced slightly, but does lift the boat by about 2 degrees. The tide sets the boat back in the first 30 minutes by about 3/4 mile. Boat B tacks for the mark after 45 minutes when well into the bay.

Meanwhile, boat A which tacked 15 minutes beforehand onto port tack for the mark, is having a difficult time. Not only is a 2½-knot tidal stream setting her away from the mark, but because the tide and the wind are acting in virtually the same direction, the apparent wind (see wind diagram) has been reduced by about 2½ knots. This reduces the speed of the boat by 1 knot through the water, to 4 knots. With the tide acting virtually in line with the wind, there is no change in wind direction and therefore the boat is neither headed or lifted.

Boat A carries on this port tack for an hour. With the boat only making 4 knots through the water and the tide running at 2 to 2½ knots, the boat is set significantly away from the mark and ends up, after 90 minutes, on the line between the two marks and only 1½ miles nearer the windward mark than when she started. Not a very good result for 90 minutes' hard sailing!

Meanwhile, boat B carries on with her starboard tack for a further 45 minutes. In the bay, the tide is running in roughly the same direction as the apparent wind generated by true wind and boat speed; this reduces slightly the 'boat' component of the triangle and gives a tidally corrected apparent wind which is closer to the true wind. The result of this is that the boat is lifted by about 3 degrees.

Boat B plugs away into the tide on the starboard tack, still going at 5 knots since the apparent wind

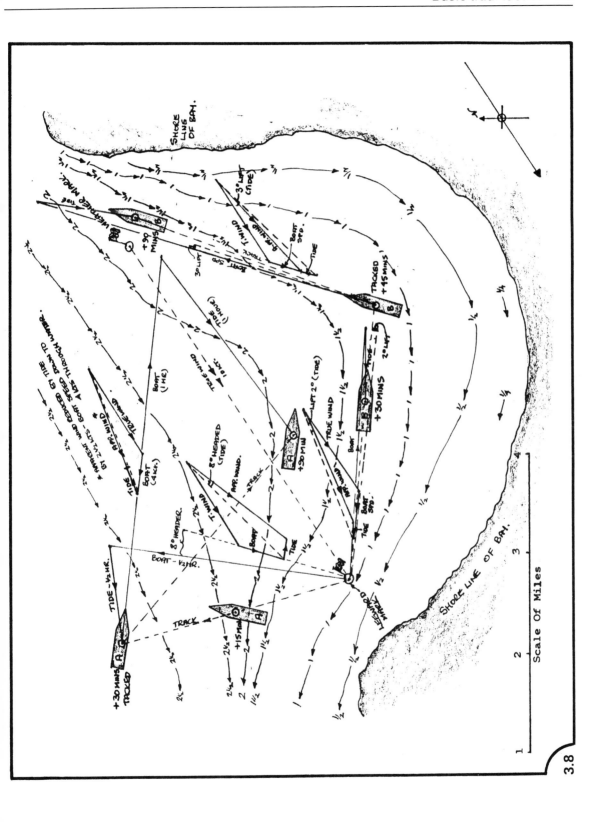

Scale Of Miles

3.8

They may well suppose that they are going to end up very close to the weather mark. It is obviously important to appreciate what the tide and the wind will do, not only for the first tack but for subsequent tacks. So many times in ocean racing, two boats do different things both of which appear eminently sensible at first. However (as in this case) when the race ends, one of the boats has gained a very significant advantage over the other, and yet their actual boat-for-boat performance may be very similar in normal circumstances. I will be giving actual examples of this later. Suffice to say that in this example boat B is 2½ miles ahead of boat A after 90 minutes on a 4-mile leg.

Pre-race planning

If you have read this far, I hope you will be able to decide what tide to expect on different parts of the course. I have tried to illustrate that the effects of tidal streams on boats racing on different parts of the course but going towards the same mark, are predictable long before the race commences. If you have an idea in which direction the wind will be blowing on the day of the race (from the previous night's forecast) then you can form as good an opinion as the race officer as to where the marks will be laid. Remember to look for the shallower patches because the committee boats and the buoys have to be anchored! Set out your own Olympic triangle as if you were the race officer, the night before. You can find the lengths of the legs in the sailing instructions. Draw your tides and tidal streams on the chart as you predict them. Then have a look at figure 3.8 as well as mumbling to yourself the various tactical rules that are outlined in this chapter. If you go through the whole somewhat laborious process, it is guaranteed that you will have far more idea of the pros and cons of the various courses on the day of the race than any of the other contestants. This advice, of course, is even more important in offshore races where the courses are fixed months before.

is not materially reduced by the tide, and after 45 minutes (having sailed 90 minutes in all) is ready to tack around the weather mark, completing the first leg of the course.

Summary

Figure 3.8 is rather complex but it can be followed if each boat's movements are looked at separately. It is arguable that the course steered by boat A is ridiculous, and no one would actually go in this direction. Admittedly (and for ease of presentation), the latter has been somewhat simplified in the drawing, but this kind of split tacking duel in a bay has happened many times (especially in Torbay, Poole Bay and at Porto Cervo, Sardinia) in national and international class races.

Look again at the position of boat A after 30 minutes: unless the helmsman had a very clear picture of the course he might well argue that he was making better progress than boat B, which at that stage has not made very much progress away from the mark into the bay. Boat A actually loses tremendously on the second (port) tack, but this may well not be apparent to her helmsman/tactician when she tacks after 30 minutes' sailing.

4   Racing on the Olympic triangle

The Olympic triangle is a course designed to alternate all points of sailing, and is used in open water with buoys especially laid for the race. A typical Olympic course is shown in figure 4.1.

In this example the windward leg (first leg) is 3 miles long and the second and third legs (starboard gybe and port gybe) are 2.12 miles long. The first three legs of the course form an isosceles triangle. The windward leg can be 1, 2, or 3 miles long (for smaller boats) or 4 or 5 miles long for larger boats. Buoys can be passed on either side, giving a left-hand course or a right-hand course. After the windward mark is passed, boats head out to the gybe mark and then come back to the leeward mark near the original start, thus completing the first round of the course. The second round of the course consists of one more windward leg and then a downwind leg back to the leeward mark, with a final windward leg to the finish up by the windward mark. This is the conventional Olympic triangle; it is set in open water and biased on the direction of the wind.

Pre-start checks

It is important to get out on the start line at least half an hour before your class is scheduled to start. As soon as the line is laid its bearing should be ascertained by looking along a hand-bearing compass when in line with the committee boat and outer mark. As well as a calculation of wind bias an appreciation of tide bias should be made. The easiest way to do this is to observe the tide around the mark buoy or committee boat. Try to get a bearing on this tide and compare it with what you expected. Remember that with a light tidal stream and a strong wind the committee boat may be wind-rode as opposed to tide-rode. In yachts it may be feasible to drop a kedge and measure the speed of the tide by log. You should, of course, have assessed the tidal speed before the race.

Starting

There are really only three possibilities on the start line. Since the course is generally laid with

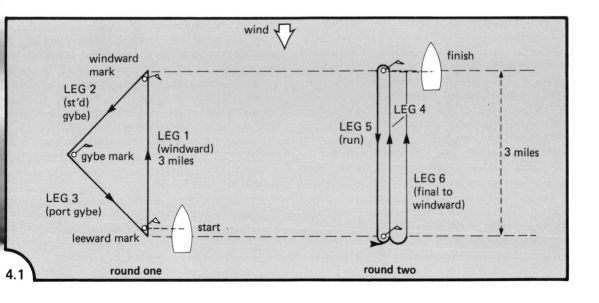

4.1

respect to the wind, the tide may be at any angle across the course, but these resolve into:

- Starting against the tide.
- Starting with the tide.
- Starting with the tide coming predominantly from one side or the other.

Starting against the tide

In the start in figure 4.2 the tide will cause each boat to take longer to reach the line than would have been anticipated, because its main effect is to make each boat 'crab' along sideways as it goes on either tack. Most boats will start on starboard tack, and therefore may well be pushed further to the port end of the line than would be the case with no tidal stream. It is therefore worth considering coming in very late by the committee boat at the starboard end of the line, and allowing the tide to keep your boat back. In figure 4.2 boat A has let her sails flap some time before the start. When she eventually comes onto the wind and begins sailing she will be in position C at the port end of the line. The group of boats in position B will similarly be pushed along the line to the original position of boat A. There is a chance that boat D will be able to go round the stern of the committee boat and start in the windward position on starboard tack.

Another consideration is that boats in general will misjudge the strength of the tidal stream and be late on the line because they have been pushed back unknowingly. This effect is more pronounced in the middle of the line than it is at the end of the line, because at either end there is a mark to give a reference. This 'tidal bulge' is illustrated in figure 4.3. The important thing is to be in the position of boat E. How is this to be achieved?

1 Before the start of the race take a transit on some shore object (identify two objects in line when the boat is on the start line) – take a bearing of this transit if possible. When you are starting in the middle of the start line this transit will tell you where the boat is in relation to the start line, even if the committee boat and the outer mark are temporarily obscured. Try to pick a transit which is above the level of the other boats' sails.

2 Do one or two timed runs to the start line, and rely on time to help you estimate where you are on the start line. Remember that if you let your sails flap you will tend to 'crab' along the line but the tide will prevent you from being swept over it.

It is thus possible to get much closer to the start line for a start against the tidal stream than would otherwise be the case.

Starting with very light winds. If the winds are so light that progress cannot be made against the tidal stream then the race start will probably be postponed. However, it is worth remembering that with very light winds combined with a strong tidal stream against the windward leg, it can take a very long time indeed to get up to the start line. In these circumstances it is probably best to stay more or less on the line during the last five minutes before the start, controlling the position of your boat by tacking and letting the sails flap so that you do not sail over the line before the start. Many instances are recorded of boats in these conditions starting up to five minutes after the official start of the race due to their inadvertently letting themselves drift too far downtide for the start.

Starting with the tidal stream

In figure 4.4 the tidal stream is pushing the boats towards the wind (increasing their apparent wind, and therefore their speed). The effect is the opposite of the example above. Boats tend to get pushed to the right when on the starboard tack. This will tend to create a bunch at position B (by the committee boat), and there is a good argument for letting the tide push your boat around the outer mark in clear water. This is the opposite of the argument for starting around the stern of the committee boat which was recommended for starting against the tide.

Bear in mind that the apparent wind will be increased; more importantly, all the boats will be pushed over the line. Your approach to the line is going to be very much faster. Again, the use of transits and a prior timed run is essential. If a 'bulge' in the line occurs, the boats will be over the line, and this situation will be exacerbated if winds are light and tidal stream strong. It is unlikely that any race committee would postpone a race in these circumstances unless the wind were practically non-existent. In light winds there is therefore a very real danger of being pushed over the line and even with a spinnaker up being unable to regain the line in time for the start. The cardinal rule in these circumstances is to have the kedge handy, and if necessary kedge on the line

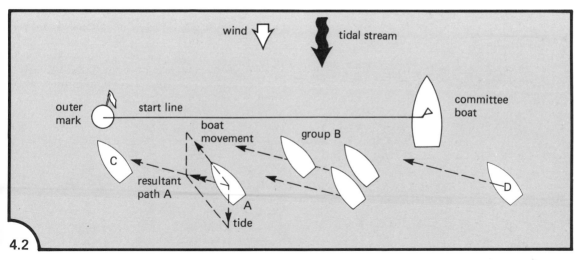

4.2

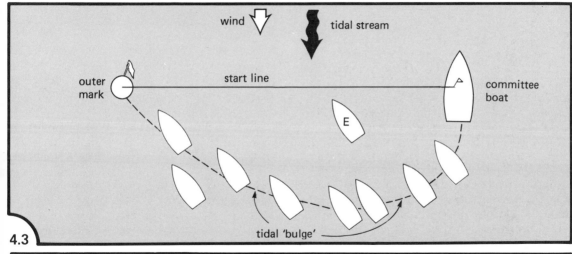

4.3

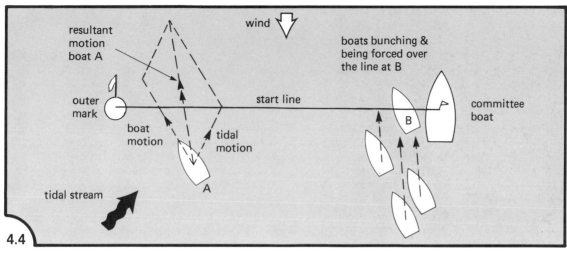

4.4

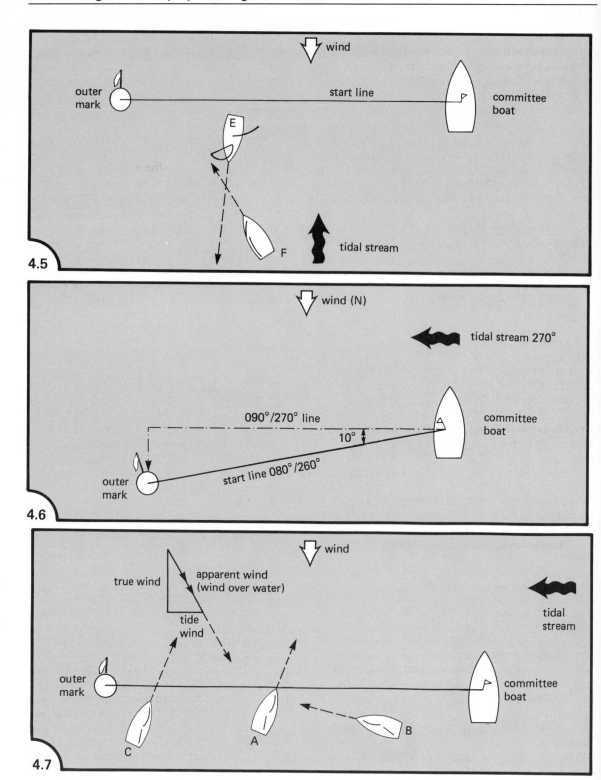

wind

outer mark

start line

committee boat

E

F   tidal stream

4.5

wind (N)

tidal stream 270°

090°/270° line

10°

committee boat

outer mark

start line 080°/260°

4.6

wind

true wind

apparent wind (wind over water)

tide wind

tidal stream

outer mark

committee boat

C

A

B

4.7

until the start (pointing in the opposite direction to the windward mark!). The worst possible start to a race is to be left attempting to get behind the start line while every other boat is going away downtide towards the windward mark, with an increased apparent wind.

Strong tidal streams. Boat E in figure 4.5 is running away from the line on the starboard gybe. Boat F is close-hauled on the starboard tack approaching the line with the tide pushing her down rapidly. Boat F has the right of way – this is a big problem for boat E. Avoid getting into boat E's difficulty by observing the following rules for strong tide/ weak wind conditions with a tidal stream pushing over the start line.

- *Either* kedge on the line; *or*
- Make careful timed runs (and take transits) well before the start, then stay well back to give yourself room for manoeuvre. Make your run for the line – probably from the left-hand side on starboard tack – fairly late.

In larger boats position-keeping before the start can be assisted by keeping the engine running until the five-minute gun and motoring to the position required. Transits may be taken on approaching the line, and the times taken between transits to give an idea of the time the boat will take to get to the start (and then you can either slow down or speed up if possible). Remember that if all else fails, stay between the outer mark and the committee boat, since if the wind drops the tide will push you over the start line and at least your boat will have made the correct start. To be pushed on the wrong side of either mark is very dangerous for obvious reasons.

Tidal stream across the course line

The extreme case of tidal bias is the tide along the start line, i.e. at 90 degrees to the wind. More usually the tide will be at an angle to the start line, and if this is so the effect of tidal bias must be allowed for in conjunction with the effects previously described (i.e. the tide with the wind or directly opposed to it).

It should be noted that occasionally race committees offset the start line slightly to allow for tidal stream, so that it carries a wind bias (in other words the start line is not at right angles to the line of the windward mark, and either the

outer mark or the committee boat is nearer the windward mark in consequence). Your pre-start checks on the direction of the wind, the direction of the windward mark and the direction of the start line will enable you to find out if this is being done.

Figure 4.6 shows a line biased to the tide. The wind is blowing from the north and the normal start line would be laid east/west. However, there is a tidal stream towards the west and to allow for this the left-hand mark (outer mark) has been set back in a southerly direction by about 10 degrees, meaning that there is a 10-degree wind bias on the line. This means that boats starting by the outer mark will actually start further from the windward mark than boats starting by the committee boat. The boats by the committee boat will be the length of the start line uptide of the other boats, which may cause a less favourable apparent wind, as detailed later.

Race committees usually do this adjustment on an arbitrary basis, and the bias is seldom intentionally more than 10 degrees.

When starting with a tidal stream across the course line there are really two main considerations.

- Starting uptide means starting significantly ahead of boats starting downtide or at the other end of the mark. This is not often an advantage, as will be explained later.
- When the tide is *not* in line with the wind the direction of the apparent wind is affected (see chapter 3).

Effect on the wind

In figure 4.7 the tidal stream is coming from the east towards the west, the wind is from the north at the top of the picture and the start line is laid in an east/west direction. Boats A, B and C are being pushed to the west by the tidal stream. The apparent wind is therefore in the direction of the dotted arrow and (as explained in the previous chapter) boat A will be freed substantially and boat B will be headed substantially. Furthermore, boat A will be pushed broadside in a westerly direction. Boat B with the tide on her starboard quarter may find it difficult even to reach the line.

There is an advantage in starting uptide, by the committee boat, but this is outweighed by the wind angle advantage gained by boats on the port tack. Only if the tidal stream is so strong and the

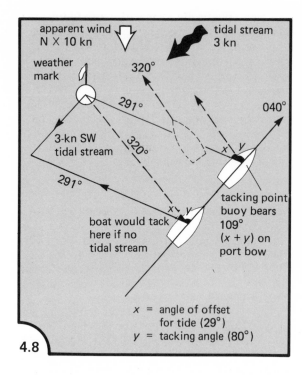

apparent wind
N × 10 kn

tidal stream
3 kn

weather
mark

320°

291°

040°

3-kn SW
tidal stream

320°

291°

x y

tacking point
buoy bears
109°
(x + y) on
port bow

boat would tack
here if no
tidal stream

x y

x = angle of offset
for tide (29°)
y = tacking angle (80°)

4.8

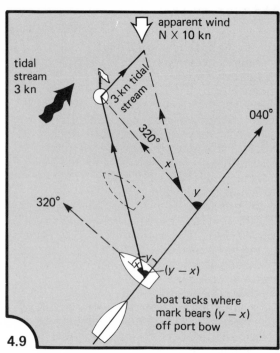

apparent wind
N × 10 kn

tidal
stream
3 kn

3-kn tidal
stream

320°

040°

x

320°

y

(y − x)

boat tacks where
mark bears (y − x)
off port bow

4.9

wind so weak as to allow the windward mark to
be gained in one tack (port tack in this case) is it
worth starting uptide. In this case (which may
develop on the windward leg, if the wind dies
away), it may be necessary to bear away against
the tide to fetch the windward mark; being uptide
from the start, and taking the port tack from the
committee boat instead of the outer mark, would
put you ahead.

So provided starboard tack is necessary to fetch
the windward mark, it is an advantage to start at
the downtide end (the outer mark in this case)
since port tack is the gaining tack, and it is
important to minimise the time the boat is on
starboard tack.

Starting can be either from the position of boat
A, which can tack onto starboard and drift down
the line towards the outer mark until the gun
goes, then go away on port near the outer mark;
or come in on port like boat C, making sure of a
clear run, and being prepared to make a short
tack to starboard while clearing the outer mark if
approached by other boats coming down the line
on starboard.

The race committee may well bias the line to
tide by moving the outer mark to the south (in
this case) to ensure the apparent wind felt by the
boats allows equal tacking with respect to the
start line. In this case, the committee boat is
closer to the windward mark than is the other end
of the line. The race committee sees it as its duty
to give a start with equal tacks, and it is important
to check the bias before the start, to see how well
they have succeeded. You will then be able to
formulate for yourself the best starting position
and pre-start tactics.

Simple rules for starting
- With a cross tide, always start at the downtide
  end unless you can make the windward mark
  on one tack, or you think the wind may go
  light (or the tidal stream increase) and the
  whole fleet may be swept downtide of the
  windward mark.
- Check the direction in which the line is laid,
  and try to work out if the race committee
  have allowed correctly for the cross tidal
  stream effect on wind. If they have not, the
  outer mark is an even better place to start
  (unless it has been set too far back!).

The windward leg

Having started correctly it is to be hoped that you are now well ahead of the fleet. If the tidal stream is against you then you will want to find that part of the course where it is weakest. If the tidal stream is with you then you will want to find that part of the course where it is strongest and sail there. Careful observation of other competing boats may give you an idea of this effect, but the best idea should come from your pre-race preparation.

If the wind is failing or the tidal stream increasing, consideration should be given to keeping uptide (all other things being equal).

If the tidal stream is with the wind, then on the windward leg frequent bearings of shore objects should be taken and the kedge should be kept ready. It is very easy for the boat to be making apparently good progress through the water but in actuality be stopped or going astern relative to the sea bed, if the adverse tidal stream is stronger than the boat's forward motion. Bearings of close objects are always the most useful indication of this, although on yachts it can be done electronically.

A bearing of the windward mark should be taken as soon as the mark can be seen. For this purpose I recommend a monocular kept around the neck with a hand-bearing compass contained in it. This aids in the identification of the windward mark (which is usually surrounded by spectator boats and race committee boats towing spare marks just to confuse the competitors) and also keeps a check on the bearing of the mark. Each time you tack, note the heading on the tack to identify windshifts and to help you estimate when to tack for the windward mark.

If the course is set in constricted waters with shoals, islands or river banks, remember to use these in the ways described in previous chapters to lessen the effect of the tide (or increase it if the stream is with you).

Approaching the weather mark

There are two main things to do on the approach to the weather mark.
- Work out when to tack from the angle of the mark.
- Work out the course to steer (allowing for tide) on the next leg.

Having the tidally corrected course to the next mark is also important to give the helmsman and sail trimmers the wind to expect on the next leg, allowing for the new course and the new boat speed. To do this requires a calculation of the true wind and the new apparent wind as well as the tidally corrected course. This is usually done on a computer or programmable calculator, but can be done on a piece of chart. It is probably beyond the scope of the dinghy sailor because of limited facilities in a small boat.

When to tack for the mark allowing for tide

Figure 4.8 shows a boat approaching the windward mark on port tack. The course that the boat will have to steer on the starboard tack to round the windward mark will be a course corrected for the tidal stream as described in the previous chapter. This can be done either by calculator, Young's Course Corrector, or on the chart. In the figure angle x is the tidal offset which is 29 degrees, and this is added to the tacking angle (y), which is 80 degrees, to give the angle off the port bow (x + y) which the windward mark must bear for a tack to round that mark to be successful. If the angle on the bow is more than the sum of these two angles the boat will have to free off on the starboard tack to round the mark, if the angle on the bow is less then the boat will not lay the mark on starboard.

In figure 4.9 the tidal stream is in the other direction and is pushing the boat past the mark. To tack successfully for the mark, the angle that the mark must bear on the bow is angle x (the tacking angle) *minus* angle y (the offset angle). The tacking angle can be estimated as the angle through which the boat has been tacking on the windward leg – that is why it is important to measure this angle after every tack. Young's Course Corrector is a very convenient instrument to use as it gives the offset angle instantly.

Armed with the tacking angle, the boat's heading and the above calculation, it is an easy matter to observe the mark with a hand-bearing compass and give the helmsman the precise moment to tack to lay the windward mark perfectly. This method is *much* to be preferred to that of the experienced sailor exercising his judgement. Very seldom does this kind of judgement allow for the tidal stream!

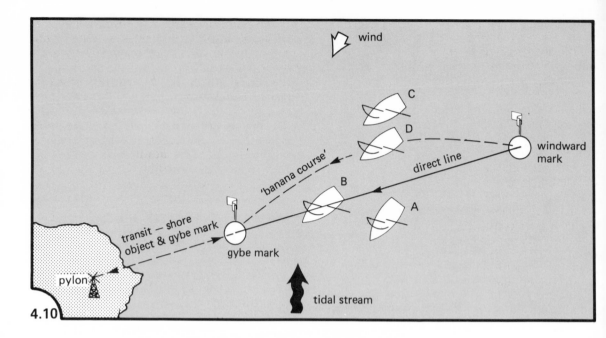

4.10

Course past the windward mark

It is essential to know what course to steer on the next leg (in this case out to the gybe mark). You should know the magnetic bearing of the gybe mark from the windward mark and the predicted tidal stream or current. Use Young's Course Corrector (or a similar instrument) or draw the vectors on the chart (see chapter 3) to find the offset angle and consequently the next course. Knowing the course well in advance means preparations can be made to trim the sails, especially on a large boat; it is also helpful for the helmsman to get the course in his head before the inevitable confusion at the windward mark as all the boats aim for one small piece of water.

It is important to give the mark a wide berth if the tidal stream is sweeping the boats onto the mark. If the tidal stream is sweeping the boats away from the mark then it is safe to go as close as possible.

Taking a transit on the next mark

As soon as the windward mark is rounded the gybe mark should be identified and a bearing taken of it. The helmsman should be steering the tidally corrected course. The shortest distance between the two marks is a straight line, and to ensure that the boat remains on that line it is necessary to observe an object on the shore behind the gybe mark as early as possible and keep the gybe mark in transit with the object by making minor adjustments to the heading. In this way the course steered will be along the line of shortest distance.

In figure 4.10 boats C and D have been swept below the straight line between the two marks by the tidal stream and are sailing a 'banana' course. Boat A is not taking a transit and is therefore stemming the tide and going above the line between the two marks and thereby going slower. Boat B has its transit and is travelling direct, and will therefore round the gybe mark ahead of the other boats.

Golden rule: wherever you are racing with a tidal stream across the course, when you are sailing directly for a mark establish a transit as soon as possible on a fixed object beyond the mark (or in default, keep a constant bearing on the approach).

Electronic instrumentation

Now that rule 12 has been relaxed, larger boats may use electronic systems such as Hercules and Decca, as well as powerful calculators or computers, which will enable them to calculate the true wind, the wind on the next leg allowing for the tidally corrected course, and other useful things which can be pre-programmed. Dinghies and smaller boats do not have this advantage. It is worth mentioning here, however, that when sailing an Olympic course all three points can be programmed into a Decca set (or similar radio/hyperbolic system) as way points with a bearing and distance from the committee boat, and the set will then indicate the true (or magnetic, depending on model) bearing and distance to any mark from the yacht. If these plotted positions are correct then the bearing of the next mark should remain constant in just the same way as a transit should remain constant. For inshore racing when visibility is bad or no suitable transit is available or for offshore work, this is a method worth considering.

The run

Having completed the two gybe legs and the next windward leg, and rounded the windward mark for the second time, it is necessary to hoist a spinnaker again and run down to the leeward mark. Depending on the characteristics of your boat it is probably best to tack downwind (i.e. keep the wind about 130 degrees on either quarter and gybe when necessary to round the leeward mark on the correct side).

It is important to get in the stronger tidal stream if it is favourable or behind the boat, and into the weaker tidal stream if it is adverse or ahead of the boat. *Tide ahead* means a stronger apparent wind (because the boat's progress is slow), and *tide astern* means less apparent wind on the run (because the boat is travelling through the water away from the wind). This is illustrated in previous chapters. Other than knowing tidal gradients across the course and watching the bearings of other boats which may have split gybes, as well as looking at variations caused by shallow patches, river eddies, etc. there is little more that one can do when the tidal stream is in line with the wind. However, with a cross tide the matter becomes more interesting.

In figure 4.11, which is similar to figure 3.5 in the previous chapter, it can be seen that the apparent wind generated by a cross-tidal stream on the run will be *towards* the source of the tidal stream. If the top of the figure is regarded as north and the tide is going from west to east, the apparent wind has veered from north to 030. Port

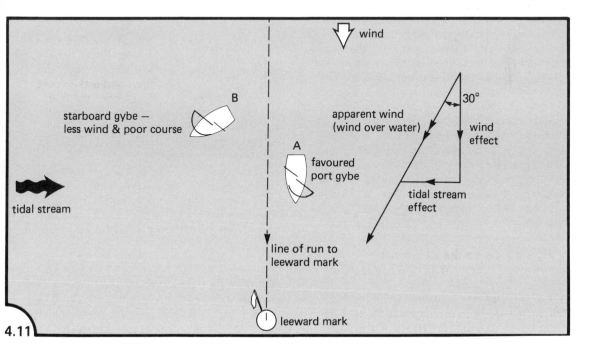

wind

B
starboard gybe —
less wind & poor course

apparent wind
(wind over water)

30°

wind
effect

A
favoured
port gybe

tidal stream
effect

tidal stream

line of run to
leeward mark

leeward mark

4.11

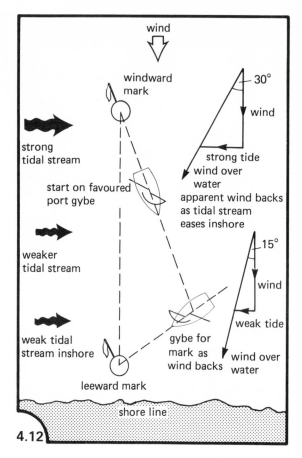

windward
mark

30°

wind

strong
tidal stream

start on favoured
port gybe

strong tide
wind over
water
apparent wind backs
as tidal stream
eases inshore

weaker
tidal stream

15°

wind

weak tide

weak tidal
stream inshore

gybe for
mark as
wind backs

wind over
water

leeward mark

shore line

4.12

then leave the second gybe (the least favoured one) as late as possible, so that the weaker tide has less adverse effect (figure 4.12).

The rule is to use the favourable downwind gybe in the stronger tide, and if an unfavourable gybe is necessary wait until the tide is weakest to take it. At all times, bearings of boats on the other gybe should be taken to ensure your strategy is correct.

Coming up to the finish

After the leeward mark has been rounded the Olympic course is completed by a final beat to the finish mark, which is usually adjacent to the original windward mark.

Approach to the finish

If the tidal stream is against you (i.e. in the same direction as the wind) there is very little you can do to gain an advantage. If the tidal stream is with the boat (i.e. 180 degrees opposed to the wind), again it makes little difference which end of the finish line you choose, although you must be careful not to tack for the finish mark too late lest your boat be swept past the finish mark and you have to free off to round it. This is illustrated in figure 4.13. In this figure boat A is making a correct approach to the finish line allowing for tide. Boat B is too far outside the outer mark. Boat A just makes the outer mark, whereas boat B is forced to free off to round it, thereby finishing astern of boat A. The rule here is – be careful not to overstand when the tide is pushing you onto the finish mark. The method for deciding when to tack for a mark applies also to this problem – although with a long finish line it is possible to make a judgement for the middle of the line which allows for reasonable error. There is no necessity to round either mark as closely as a turning mark.

Finishing across the tidal stream

When the tide is across the wind, both the shift of apparent wind and the set of the tide turn the last windward leg into 'long and short' tacks. In figure 4.14 the tide is flowing from east to west and the wind is north, port tack is the long gaining tack and starboard tack is the losing tack. Boat B in figure 4.14 on port will go much faster than boat A which started on starboard. Not only is the tide

gybe is therefore favoured. Not only is the wind automatically on A's port quarter, but because tidal stream is pushing her into the new apparent wind, the wind across the deck is increased. Also the course made good is towards the leeward mark.

On the run there is always a favoured gybe, but it may not be so favoured as to take the boat to the leeward mark in one tack or leg.

Because of the incidence of sea breezes the windward mark is often laid offshore and the leeward mark inshore. This usually means crossing tidal streams which are weaker inshore than they are offshore, thus introducing a tidal gradient along the course. On the run it is most important to leave the windward mark on the favoured gybe as described above. If it is apparent that the leeward mark will not be reached in one gybe,

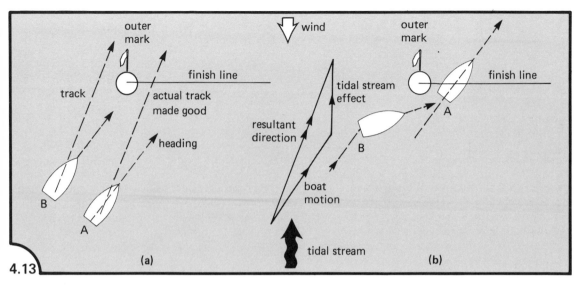

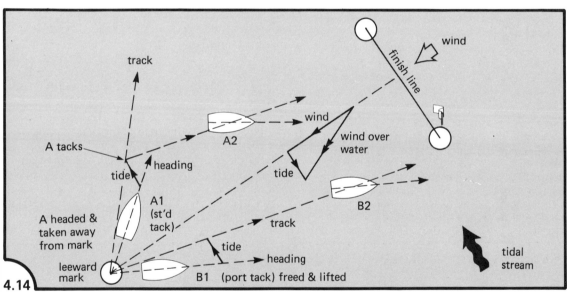

pushing B into the wind (lee bowing) and therefore increasing its apparent wind, but B is freed by the apparent wind backing due to the tidal stream. Boat A, on starboard, has been headed and slowed. Moreover, in spite of the fact that boat B is heading well to starboard of the finish line the tidal stream is pushing her up and it will be simple to judge a short starboard tack to finish.

Conversely, it is almost impossible to judge from the leeward mark how long the starboard tack should be. This leads to the following rules.

- When starting or rounding the leeward mark in a cross tide, always go away on the favoured tidal tack as soon as possible after the rounding or the start.
- In a cross tide always aim for the uptide end of the finish line.

Bearings and transits can assist with laying the uptide end of the finish line. Remember that the favoured tack will always take you over the line quicker, but don't forget boat for boat tactics right at the end of the race.

5 Inshore racing

An inshore race differs from an Olympic triangle in several respects. It may be started from a shore transit and outer mark (such as the most famous, the starting platform of the Royal Yacht Squadron at Cowes), which means that the first leg of the race is not necessarily to windward.

The race is defined with reference to existing navigational buoys in the main, although occasionally a windward mark is laid by the race committee to assist in getting a large fleet away from the start. Navigational buoys are passed in the order laid out in the race instructions, either to port or to starboard, and the course usually consists of two or three rounds which may comprise different existing navigational marks for each round.

The finish line may be defined with reference to a shore transit, usually the starting platform of a waterside yacht club.

Tidal features of the inshore race

Possibly the most celebrated area for inshore races is the Solent. Figure 5.1 shows the tidal streams of the Solent one hour before high water at Portsmouth. It is easy to see that the tidal streams are very different in the west of the Solent, where a very slight ebb is flowing, from those in the east of the Solent, where the tide is flooding in towards Southampton quite strongly.

An inshore race which ranges over a large area is therefore likely to provide a big variation in tide. Large boats ahead of a fleet will tend to be in a different tidal stream to the smaller boats astern. Further, when more than one round of a course is sailed, the tidal streams experienced on the second and subsequent rounds are likely to be completely different from those experienced during the first round. It is vital to be able to predict what is happening at each mark at each time of rounding.

Depth

Inshore races are run in estuaries and creeks where there are mudbanks, rocks and shoals. An Olympic triangle is always laid clear of the shallows, but an inshore race usually offers a choice of course when going from one navigational mark to the next. This means that the fleet will generally split up around shoals, each group trying to avoid adverse tidal stream.

Hugging the shore usually means that the boat

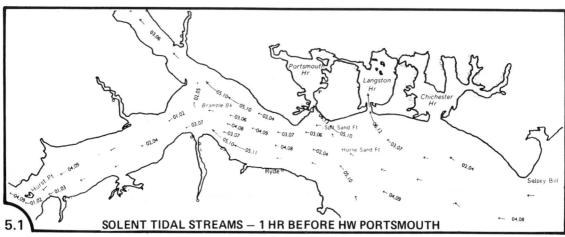

5.1 SOLENT TIDAL STREAMS — 1 HR BEFORE HW PORTSMOUTH

Based upon British Admiralty Charts with the permission of the Controller of HM Stationery Office and of the Hydrographer of the Navy

that gains most advantage is next to the boat that runs aground. More of this later.

Pre-race preparation

Race instructions are usually issued which give a choice of courses and a small chart showing the buoys in the area in which the race will be sailed.

Usually in the race instructions each buoy has a designating letter or figure to make the signalling of the course possible by the use of six or eight letters (designating the marks coded in the programme). Alternatively the programme may contain a list of courses (which is a consecutive list of buoys with an indication of which side each must be passed), each course having its own number, and the course to be sailed is signalled to the fleet (usually at the five-minute gun), merely by displaying the appropriate number.

The exact course to be sailed is therefore not usually known until five minutes before the start, although sometimes flags are shown to indicate whether the start will be to the east or the west. Your race preparation will split into three parts, namely:

- General preparation on tides and tidal streams in the area.
- Investigation into the tides and tidal streams in the area of the known start line.
- Specific preparation for the course. This will have to be done as the race proceeds; most

can be done on the first leg, in the larger boats.

General preparation for a race in tidal waters, and the tidal preparation for the start, have been covered in previous chapters. It is important to be on the start line well before the race commences, and if other classes are starting prior to your own, the opportunity should be taken to observe which way they are being sent off, and what tactics seem to be paying off.

Remember that for larger boats an inshore race may be up to forty miles long and will take perhaps seven hours in light conditions. There is plenty of time therefore to develop both tidal and other tactics as the race progresses. Indeed it would not be possible to pre-plan tactics for the whole race prior to the start.

The start

Depending on the size of the boat, you should have with you your charts, your tide tables and your tidal atlases duly pencilled in. If possible have a Young's Course Corrector, a programmable calculator, a good hand-bearing compass (or preferably a monocular or binocular with a hand-bearing compass inset into it). Know where and when the tide will turn, and where it will turn first.

If the start is to be from a fixed platform it will

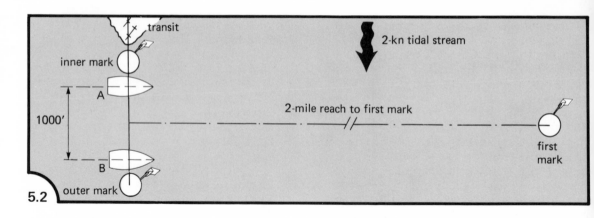

5.2

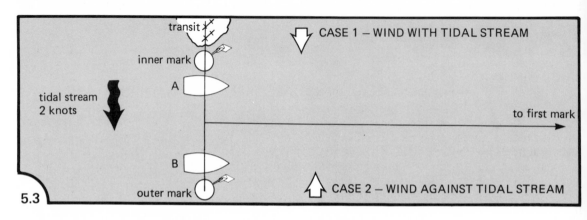

5.3

possibly not be a pure windward start. In general, race committees try to start each fleet on a beat or a reach if possible. However running starts are not unknown, and so it is important to look at the start of an inshore race in more detail. These remarks also apply to offshore races which are started in a similar manner.

An upwind start with a tidal stream has been dealt with in the previous chapter. A reaching start is a fairly simple matter wherever the tide is, since all boats will be on a similar heading. With a constant wind across the start line, it is usually best to start in the strongest favourable tidal stream or weakest adverse tidal stream.

Reaching start – cross tidal stream
In figure 5.2 it is 2 miles to the first mark, and the tidal stream is setting southerly across the course to the first mark which is east/west. If we allow the average speeds of all the boats to be about 6 knots on the reach, then it will take 20 minutes to

cover the 2 miles to the first mark. In that time the tidal stream going southerly at 2 knots will have travelled 4053 ft. All boats will have to stem the tide to cover this distance before reaching the first mark. Boat A (uptide) will have 1000 ft less tide to stem than boat B on a 1000 ft course line (3553 ft to stem as opposed to 4553 ft).

In figure 5.3 the tidal stream is southerly at 2 knots. In case 1 the wind is northerly (i.e. in the same direction as the tidal stream) and in case 2 the wind is southerly (opposed to the tidal stream). With the wind and the tide coming from the north it is obviously better to start upwind and uptide. This is the position of boat A.

With the tide opposed to the wind (in case 2) boat A will be pushed down towards the line of the first mark thus increasing her apparent wind, whereas boat B will have to turn away from the wind and stem the tide to make the first mark. This means that whichever way the wind is, it is *always* better to start uptide when on a reach.

This is really an extension of the rule outlined in the previous chapter, which is:
Golden rule – if the first mark can be gained without having to tack or gybe, then it is always better to start uptide (all other things being equal).

The running start

Just occasionally a running start will be given on an inshore or offshore race. Usually this is a method by which the race committee clears the start line between classes. However, in some cases where both the start line and the first mark are fixed, a running start becomes inevitable because of the prevailing wind.

Running start – cross tidal stream. With the tidal stream across the course the same rules should be followed as outlined on page 39 for the run leg of an Olympic triangle. In other words, the favourable gybe should be identified and selected at the start.

Looking at figure 5.4, it is apparent that after selecting the favourable gybe it is still important to start uptide since the first mark can be reached on a single gybe. Boat A has a line of approach which approximates the first mark because the tidal stream is pushing her down on the mark from the upper end of the start line. Boat B will go well to the south of the mark unless she brings

the wind much more nearly astern or gybes before reaching the mark. If boat A risks passing to the north of the mark, then she can come harder on the wind (i.e. turn slightly to starboard) to make the mark – which is a much faster point of sailing. Two things should be remembered here:

- If the wind falls light then the whole fleet may end up partially stemming the tide, and boats uptide will have a significant advantage.
- This is a classic case of needing to take a bearing (or preferably a transit) on the first mark to make sure the course being steered is the shortest one, and a constant bearing (or transit) should be maintained on the mark as your boat approaches it.

Running start – favourable tidal stream. In figure 5.5 the tidal stream is in the same direction as the wind, and both are pushing the boats over the line. To cross the line too early (or to make the approach too early) is extremely dangerous. Getting back behind the line would entail dropping the spinnaker, hoisting the genoa, beating back against wind and tide, and then turning round, hoisting the spinnaker and dropping the genoa again. All the while the rest of the fleet would be going away under favourable wind and tide towards the first mark.

The safest way to handle this situation is to

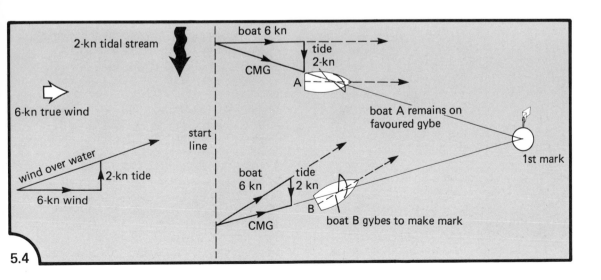

5.4

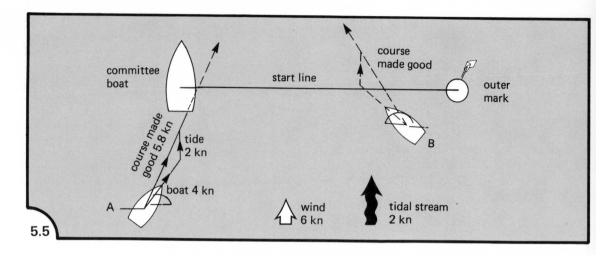

5.5

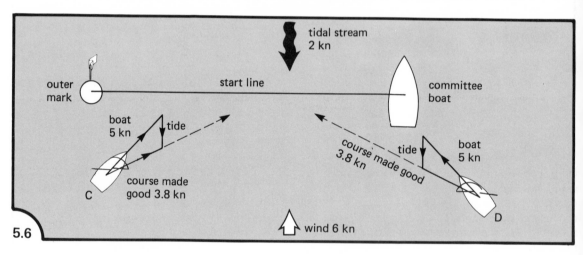

5.6

make a practice run with the spinnaker up well before the start. This run should be from a known transit and should be timed, and safety margins of perhaps fifteen seconds should be left when the actual start is being made. Don't do this after the five-minute gun, when the engine must be stopped, because of the time required (as described above) to return to the starting position. On the run in, the boat can be slowed by letting the spinnaker fly or hoisting it very late.

It is very important to take several transits and plot them on the chart against the known position of the committee boat to give an idea of distances off the line. These should be noted by the navigator and taken on deck for the run in to the start. Avoid getting in the position of boat A in

figure 5.5 for if the wind should fall light she will be swept by the tidal stream the wrong side of the committee boat, unless she kedges.

Running start – adverse tidal stream. This is a much easier problem, since by spilling wind from the sails and putting the spinnaker up at the last moment, it is possible to 'hover' on the line, stemming the tidal stream ready to put the sail power on at the critical moment just before the start. It is important not to get too far away from the start line, since if the wind falls light it may be difficult to get up to the line in time for the gun. For this reason it is important to keep the engine running (if one is carried) up to the five-minute gun.

Boat D in figure 5.6 is making the classic port-

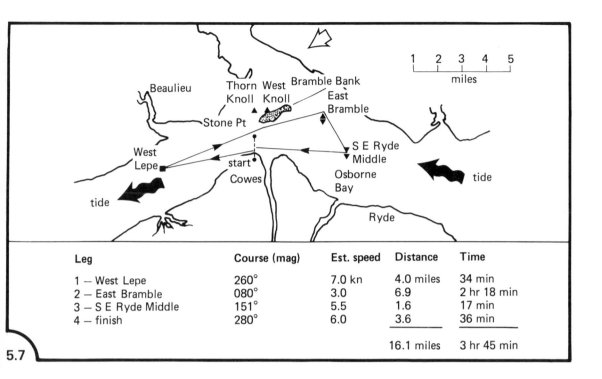

Leg	Course (mag)	Est. speed	Distance	Time
1 — West Lepe	260°	7.0 kn	4.0 miles	34 min
2 — East Bramble	080°	3.0	6.9	2 hr 18 min
3 — S E Ryde Middle	151°	5.5	1.6	17 min
4 — finish	280°	6.0	3.6	36 min
			16.1 miles	3 hr 45 min

5.7

gybe start round the stern of the committee boat, using the tidal stream to make the boat crab along to port, but generally it is probably best to start in the area of least adverse tide. Where a shore transit is used this usually means starting close to the inner mark.

The race

Figure 5.7 shows the Solent with a typical triangular course going from the Squadron line to West Lepe buoy, then out to East Bramble buoy, down to South East Ryde middle buoy and finally back to the finish on the Squadron line again. This is a fairly typical round of a Solent course. The wind is light from the east north-east, and the tidal streams are as shown in figure 5.8 for high water Portsmouth. In other words, they are flooding in the east Solent and ebbing in the west Solent.

I am going to look at this course leg by leg, discussing how you should relate your tactics to the effect of the tide at each stage.

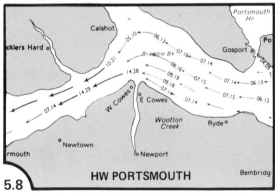

HW PORTSMOUTH

5.8

Based upon British Admiralty Charts with the permission of the Controller of HM Stationery Office and of the Hydrographer of the Navy

First leg

Both wind and tidal stream are astern of the boats, the first course being about 260 degrees magnetic to West Lepe. From figure 5.8 at spring tides it can be seen that the tidal stream is approximately 246 degrees at 2.8 knots. Allowing a boat speed of 6 knots this will give an offset of 7 degrees, so the course to steer would be

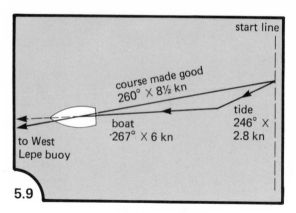

5.9

strength of the new apparent wind should be worked out to enable the correct rig to be prepared. There is a distinct danger of overrunning the mark as the tidal stream is sweeping all the boats past West Lepe buoy. As the mark is approached the helmsman should be given the new direction and since the tide will now be adverse, the boat should set off on starboard tack to get into the shore off Beaulieu where the tidal stream inshore is much weaker.

As West Lepe is rounded, observe the tidal stream on the buoy and estimate its strength and direction.

The windward leg

Both wind and tide are now against you. You must seek shelter from the tidal stream by going inshore; however, there are many shoals off Beaulieu and so the chart must be studied very carefully. If possible someone should watch the echo sounder at all times. There are areas where a deeper inlet gives way to a shallow bar which must be rounded. It is true to say that in a spring tide in the Solent the boat that goes furthest in without running aground will probably win the race.

For the first part of this leg the race will turn into a short-tacking duel with many cries for 'water'. Some daring boats will run aground, some less daring will stay too far out and be left behind. For the larger boats the optimum band is between 6 ft and 15 ft depth on the echo sounder, with a close watch being kept on the chart for lumps, bumps and shallow channels and ridges.

approximately 267 degrees to allow for the tidal stream and to make the mark (figure 5.9).

The first mark will be made on the starboard gybe and the stronger tide will be towards the outer end of the line, in the main stream. This is where the start should be made. The initial course should be set at 267 degrees and immediately a transit should be set up (or in default a bearing) on West Lepe and a shore object behind it. Remember that if the transit is lost, then a new one should be set up. No attempt should be made to regain the old transit, since the shortest distance from where you are to the mark is along the new transit (having wandered off from the original one).

Approaching the mark
The next leg will be a beat against the tide. The

Tide tote: Brambles Bank, 1 March at 1200

HW Portsmouth 1250 GMT, height 4.8 metres, range 4.4 metres (see figure 1.1)

Mean Low Water Springs (MLWS) Cowes — 0.6 m to Chart Datum; Lee on Solent — 0.8 m; Calshot — 0.6 m (from Chart 394)

AVERAGE TO CHART DATUM	+ 0.7 m deep
Shallowest patch Brambles	−(1.3 m) dries
Brambles MLWS	−(0.6 m) dries
Range to HW 1 March	+ 4.4 m
Brambles at HW 1 March	+ 3.8 m at 1250 GMT
+ 1 hour (1/12 of range)	+ 3.4 m at 1350 GMT
+ 2 hours (2/12 of range)	+ 2.7 m at 1450 GMT
+ 3 hours (3/12 of range)	+ 1.6 m at 1550 GMT

5.10   If boat draws 2.5 metres, don't cross Bramble Bank after 1500

Nerve racking, but rewarding if you get it right!

When Stone Point is rounded, the Bramble Bank bars the way to the next mark. To go south of the Bramble Bank would put your boat in the strongest adverse tide. The choice is either to go to the north of the bank or to go over the bank. A decision must be made. On a falling spring tide to run aground would be disastrous, and yet over the shallow Bramble Bank will be the weakest adverse tide in the whole of the Solent. Figure 5.10 shows a simple depth tote which the astute tidal tactician should have available, having made it out while everyone else was involved in the close tacking inshore off Beaulieu.

Having established that sufficient depth exists over the Bramble Bank for your boat, tack in an easterly line of approach over the tail of the Bramble Bank past Thorn Knoll, West Knoll and on to East Bramble buoy.

The third leg
The next leg takes us down to the South East Ryde Middle buoy. The tidal stream is running at about 300 degrees magnetic by about 1½ knots. Figure 5.11 shows the offset angle.

By the end of the second leg nearly three hours will have elapsed (see table below figure 5.7), so in reality the tidal stream would be that for 3 hours after HW Portsmouth if the start was at

HW Portsmouth. Using only one tidal atlas page we have to assume for this example the tidal stream is constant at any one place throughout the race.

This is a short leg – only 1.6 miles – and with a slight adverse tidal stream it will take about 17 minutes to cover. The previous beat against the tide, at an average 3 knots, took all of 2 hours and 18 minutes. The offset angle is about 7 degrees into the tidal stream and so the course to steer is 144 degrees magnetic. When crossing the channel in a tidal stream like this it is very important to get a bearing somewhere in Ryde, to make sure that the transit on the South East Ryde Middle buoy remains constant.

The final leg to the finish
Figure 5.12 shows the last leg. The tidal stream is weak in Osborne Bay at only 1.4 knots (at springs) and is stronger at HW Portsmouth across Ryde Middle Sand. It is stronger still, however, in the main channel to the north of Ryde Middle Sand. Which is the fastest course back to the finish from South-East Ryde Middle buoy?

All boats will sail this leg on the starboard gybe as shown. Boat B elects to sail up over the Ryde Middle Sand towards the stronger tidal stream. Initially this is a faster point of sailing obtained by bringing the apparent wind further forward. Boat A sails along the direct line between the South-East Ryde Middle and the finish. As soon as boat B gets into the stronger tidal stream she will pull ahead. Although towards the end boat A will be sailing closer to the wind (and therefore faster) than boat B, which will have to free off to pass inside the outer limit mark on the finish line transit, nonetheless boat B will have a significant tidal advantage. This might be an average of 0.2 knot for 36 minutes, or 730 ft (20 boat lengths) which will enable B to finish ahead. The outer end of the finish line, with its stronger favourable tidal stream, is the place to finish.

How far should you deviate in order to get a stronger tidal stream? There is no definite answer on this; it is a matter of judgement. Factors on which you should base your decision are the likely time on the leg (see the table under figure 5.7); the tidal difference from one part of the course to the other; and the likely gain obtained by going across a tidal gradient into a stronger favourable tide (or into a weaker adverse tide).

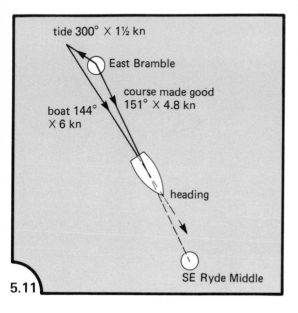

tide 300° X 1½ kn

East Bramble

course made good
151° X 4.8 kn

boat 144°
X 6 kn

heading

SE Ryde Middle

5.11

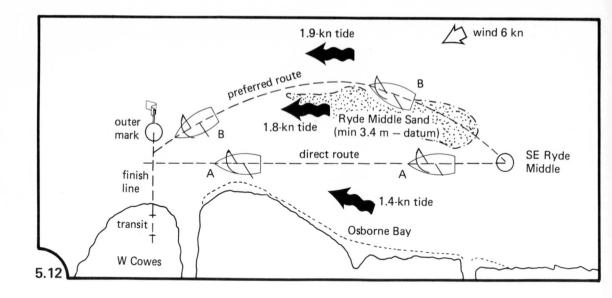

5.12

Time on the leg is most important – this will vary with the angle of sailing and the wind strength. The longer your boat will spend sailing the leg, the more worthwhile it will be to deviate into more favourable (or less adverse) tide.

In light winds, in a beat against an adverse tide (as with the West Lepe to East Bramble leg) very large deviations to avoid the main adverse tidal stream are generally worthwhile. On a much quicker run back such as the final leg of this race, a gentle loop into the more favourable tidal stream is all that is needed.

Remember that if your boat is in the most favourable tide – even if it is only by 50 metres or so – it is gaining an advantage, so keep well uptide of the fleet in a situation like this.

Conclusion

The tidal rules of the inshore race are as follows and should be committed to memory.

1 Make sure you have done your preparation before the race.

2 Make sure you have all your equipment on board.

3 Get to the start line very early.

4 Watch other classes start to ascertain the paying tactic.

5 Plan the start carefully. Everyone will be checking on the wind; make sure you take the tide into consideration as well.

6 Draw on the courses and measure the distances as soon as possible, and make sure that any shallow areas (such as the south Bramble shoal) are carefully looked at, and if necessary a tote of depth against time produced.

7 Take a transit or bearing on each buoy as you approach it.

8 Make sure the helmsman knows the correct course allowing for tidal stream well before rounding the buoy.

9 Make sure you know the angle at which to tack for each buoy, allowing for the tidal offset.

10 Observe each buoy you pass to give an idea of tidal stream and variations on different parts of the course.

11 If the fleet splits, take bearings of the other boats to make sure that yours is the correct strategy and that other boats are not gaining on you in another part of the course.

12 On a leg where an option exists to go into a different tidal stream, try to weigh up the benefits using judgements based on time on leg, wind strength and tidal gradient to decide on the most favourable deviation from the straight line between the marks.

6 Offshore racing

This chapter looks at tidal strategy in offshore and ocean races. Much of what we have learned in previous chapters will apply but some aspects are completely different from an inshore race. The easiest way to cover this subject is to use a real-life example illustrated with notes and diagrams from the navigator's note book.

The event I have chosen is the De Guingand Bowl race of 1983 which commenced off Cowes on Friday 13 May and finished early on Sunday 15 May off Gilkicker Fort, in the Solent.

I was at the time navigating the Class 1 yacht 'Yeoman XXIII' which won the De Guingand Bowl race outright as you will see. The primary reason for this win was a correct appreciation of tidal strategy, which in practice meant going in a different direction from the rest of the fleet.

Sailing instructions

With an offshore race, the start, the course and the finish are known well before the race commences, and so it is possible to do a great amount of the pre-race preparation at home well before the start. In this particular race the start was off the Squadron Line at Cowes, then through the Forts in the eastern Solent, out to the Nab Tower which was rounded to starboard, across to CH1 buoy (the fairway buoy for Cherbourg Harbour) which would be rounded to starboard, back to the Poole Bar buoy (again rounded to starboard), round the Isle of Wight leaving St Catherine's Point and Bembridge Ledge buoy to port, through the Forts again and then three miles to the Royal Ocean Racing Club's finish line set up on Fort Gilkicker. Figure 6.1 shows

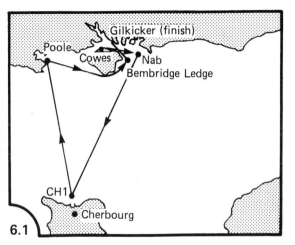

6.1

Navigation notes for the de Guingand Bowl race					
Start: Cowes line at 2010 BST (class 1)					
Run	Course (magnetic)	Distance (miles)	Cuml. distance	ETA 6 kn	ETA 7½ kn
Cowes – Forts	112°	8	8	Fri 1830	Fri 2114
Forts – Nab	136°	8	16	Fri 2250	Fri 2218
Nab – CH1	215°	63	79	Sat 0920	Sat 0642
CH1 – Poole	358°	56	135	Sat 1840	Sat 1410
Poole – St Catherine's	108°	23	158	Sat 2230	Sat 1714
St Catherine's – Bembridge	077° 049°	5 7	170	Sun 0030	Sat 1850
Bembridge – Forts	336°	4	174	Sun 0110	Sat 1922
Forts – finish	320°	3	177	Sun 0140	Sat 1946
			177	29 hr 30 min	23 hr 36 min

6.2

Tides for race (on springs)

	Fri	Sat	Sun
Portsmouth (HW)	1236	0057	0138
		1319	1406
Dover (HW)	1206	0022	0103
		1249	1332
Cherbourg (HW)	–	0946	–

NB: start on flood 5 hours before HW.
Starts to ebb about midnight (on way to CH1).
Floods again about 0600 on Saturday (gate at CH1?).
   All times are BST.

6.3

the course in diagrammatic form, and figure 6.2 is a copy of the navigator's log book. This indicates the start at Cowes at 2010 BST, with the run, the course, the distance, the cumulative distance, and the estimated time of arrival (ETA) at each point at both 6 knots and 7½ knots. At the bottom the total distance can be noted (177 miles) and under the time columns, the elapsed times. This kind of tote is always recommended as an initial framework for tackling the tactics of the race.

Tides
The next table to produce is a tote of tides, and this is shown in figure 6.3. The three days of the race (Friday, Saturday and Sunday) are on the left-hand side and then the times of high water for those days for Portsmouth, Dover and Cherbourg are shown in the columns. It is from these times of high water that the relevant pages of the tidal atlases will be completed.

A few short notes on the initial considerations are made under the tidal tote. Note that tides were at springs, and so the maximum tidal streams were expected. The start was on the flood some five hours before high water, and the tide began to ebb about midnight when the fleet was on the way to the CH1 buoy having rounded the Nab. The flood started again about 0600 on Saturday 14 May which gave rise to a tidal gate at CH1.

Tidal gates
Before this chapter is over you will hear a lot

about tidal gates. Briefly a tidal gate occurs when the leading boats round a mark with a favourable tide which then turns and makes it very difficult for smaller classes or tardy boats to round the same mark. This is known as 'shutting the gate'. Boats that round the mark with favourable tidal streams open up a huge lead on boats that have to battle against adverse streams at the same mark through having arrived later. The tidal gate is an important tactical weapon in a handicap race.

Weather
The weather forecast broadcast at 1355 on Friday 13th predicted a southerly wind, 10 to 15 knots, possibly backing a little and decreasing.

Pre-planning
All the charts for the course were required, as well as the almanac and the tidal stream atlases: for this race MP250 *English and Bristol Channels*, MP337 *The Solent and Adjacent Waters*, and MP264 *The Channel Island and Adjacent Coasts of France*. After ascertaining the times of high water at Portsmouth, Dover and Cherbourg, these atlases were filled in. The Solent atlas needed only to be filled in for the expected time of the start and three or four hours after it, and four or five hours before the finish. The atlas for the Channel Islands was for the arrival at and the departure from CH1 buoy off Cherbourg. The atlas for the English Channel was in use most of the race.

Other equipment recommended for an offshore race includes a hand-bearing compass or, better still, a binocular or monocular with a compass in it; Young's Course Corrector; and hopefully a reasonable amount of marine electronics such as a log, echo sounder, Decca Navigator, RDF and the like.

The race
The race started as planned for Class 1 at 2010 BST on the evening of Friday 13 May 1983. This approximated to 5 hours before high water at Portsmouth (actually at 0057 on Saturday – see figure 6.3). From figures 6.4 and 6.5 it is apparent that the tidal stream was going to be with the fleet at least out to the Nab Tower and then would be

fine on the starboard bow for the first part of the long run to CH1 buoy.

Before the start I briefed the crew on the wind and tide considerations for the first part of the race. It is important that foredeck hands, midship hands and certainly the helmsman should have an idea of exactly where the boat is going and not just where it is pointing.

The briefing for this part of the race followed the considerations outlined in the previous chapters for an inshore race. "With this pattern of tidal streams it is important to get into the strongest favourable tide, and with a southerly wind the run out through the Forts to the Nab Tower will be a continuous starboard reach. The strongest tidal stream flows just to the south of the Ryde Middle Bank (from inspection of the tidal atlas) and then out to the passage between the Forts. The tidal stream will come on to the starboard beam as the fleet hardens up towards the Nab Tower and a more southerly course will have to be adopted to cope with this and make good the rhumb line over the ground to pass the Nab Tower close to starboard".

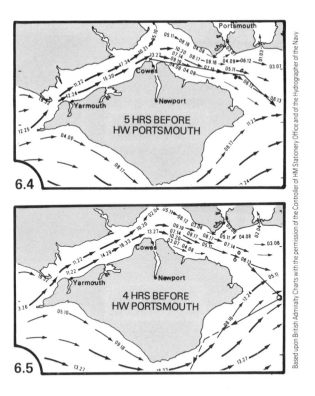

6.4 5 HRS BEFORE HW PORTSMOUTH

6.5 4 HRS BEFORE HW PORTSMOUTH

Based upon British Admiralty Charts with the permission of the Controller of HM Stationery Office and of the Hydrographer of the Navy

The first long leg to CH1

The approach to the Nab Tower was uneventful and it was rounded at 2155 BST with 'Yeoman' well up with the leaders.

The first course given to the helmsman was the rhumb line to CH1 (from figure 6.2 this is 215 degrees). Since a Decca Navigator was carried, the latitude and longitude of CH1 was put in as a way point so that a continuous display of the bearing (true) and distance to the next buoy was available on the Decca screen.

Until midnight the tidal stream came around the southern side of the Isle of Wight in an approximate southwesterly direction. Rather than set off on a starboard reach it seemed better in the southerly wind to tack onto port and get into Sandown Bay and under the cliffs at Dunnose Point on the Isle of Wight, to avoid this adverse tidal stream (figure 6.8). On port tack a substantial amount of westing was made while the tide continued to sweep in from the west. This is illustrated by the lines drawn on figure 6.5, and follows the rule about getting inshore when the tide is adverse. To have remained on the starboard tack would have meant being swept up-channel and away from the mark.

By midnight on Friday 'Yeoman', in company with other Class 1 boats, was close inshore off Dunnose Point. The tidal stream was slackening, at one hour before HW Portsmouth (0057 BST). In the nearly slack tidal stream at 2353 hrs 'Yeoman' tacked onto starboard again, and with the wind now nearly southwest made good a course of 200 degrees magnetic with 58 miles to run to CH1.

Tidal diamonds on the run across

Making a fifty or sixty-mile crossing of the Channel or a similar waterway, where in general the tidal streams run at right angles to the course outward and homeward, requires a new set of tactics. Figure 6.6 shows the tides over a nine-hour period experienced at tidal diamond N in the middle of the Channel. Figure 6.8 shows the outward leg of this race to CH1.

To cover the 58 miles from Dunnose Point to CH1 in winds which were lightening all the time would need about nine hours at an average of about 6.5 knots. Tidal streams change their direction roughly every six hours. Therefore it was important to know the *net tidal effect* over a

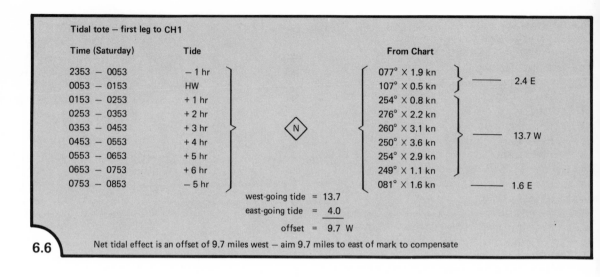

Tidal tote – first leg to CH1

Time (Saturday)	Tide	From Chart	
2353 – 0053	– 1 hr	077° × 1.9 kn	
0053 – 0153	HW	107° × 0.5 kn	} 2.4 E
0153 – 0253	+ 1 hr	254° × 0.8 kn	
0253 – 0353	+ 2 hr	276° × 2.2 kn	
0353 – 0453	+ 3 hr	260° × 3.1 kn	
0453 – 0553	+ 4 hr	250° × 3.6 kn	} 13.7 W
0553 – 0653	+ 5 hr	254° × 2.9 kn	
0653 – 0753	+ 6 hr	249° × 1.1 kn	
0753 – 0853	– 5 hr	081° × 1.6 kn	1.6 E

west-going tide = 13.7
east-going tide = 4.0
offset = 9.7 W

6.6   Net tidal effect is an offset of 9.7 miles west – aim 9.7 miles to east of mark to compensate

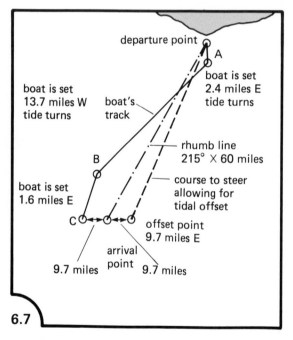

departure point

A

boat is set
2.4 miles E
tide turns

boat is set
13.7 miles W
tide turns

boat's
track

B

rhumb line
215° × 60 miles

course to steer
allowing for
tidal offset

boat is set
1.6 miles E

C

offset point
9.7 miles E

arrival
point

9.7 miles   9.7 miles

6.7

nine-hour period to enable a course to be steered which would, held steady for nine hours, put the boat on the mark.

Tidal offset in ocean races

In shorter, inshore races the course of the boat should be offset into the tide so that the rhumb line between the marks can be followed (pages 26-7). However, this assumes a constant tidal stream during the leg of the race. The rule in offshore races is usually reversed.

If the tide starts by flowing to the east, then any offset into that tidal stream would lose speed over the ground, since a certain component of the boat's motion directly opposes the tide. If the boat sails at 90 degrees to the tidal stream then it will be swept with the tide but its forward motion will be at a maximum. When the tide turns and the tidal stream runs in the other direction, the boat will be swept back towards the rhumb line – without any need to stem the tide in either direction. In practice, though, the tidal streams do not cancel each other exactly, so some offset is needed.

The rule therefore in offshore races is *not* to offset the course into the tide to stay on the rhumb line, but to work out the total tidal effect over the entire passage (allowing a reasonable speed) before deciding on the course to steer. If the boat keeps up the intended speed and the tidal streams behave as predicted, steering the offset course will put the boat on the mark at the time estimated. This is illustrated in figure 6.7 and also in figure 6.8 showing the path of 'Yeoman' on the outward leg. From figure 6.6 the total offset can be seen to be 9.7 miles to the east of CH1 buoy, since the aggregate tidal set in the nine hours across to CH1 is 9.7 miles west.

The first leg

The fleet started off on an approximate course of

200 degrees magnetic with a wind that was dying as the French coast was approached, and beginning to back slightly to the south. The positions reached by 'Yeoman' at 0453 on the Saturday morning and at 0530 are shown in figure 6.8. At 0530 it was becoming increasingly apparent that the backing, dying wind, as well as the end of the west-going tide, gave a danger of being caught downtide when the flood started somewhere around 0800, and therefore it was decided to tack onto port. At 0630 'Yeoman' tacked back onto starboard, and again tacked at 0711 in almost slack tide to round CH1 at 0838 on Saturday morning. At this time the wind had almost died completely and visibility was poor. At that stage we were leading the fleet by about fifteen minutes. The tide then began to flood strongly off Cherbourg and subsequent boats found it increasingly difficult to round CH1 in the very light wind. Thus the first of several tidal gates in this race was created.

Lessons from the first leg

1 Do all the preparation well in advance so that you have some idea of what is likely to happen, in the first half of the race at least.

2 Brief the crew adequately to give them an idea of the tactics.

3 Make sure that by selecting a convenient diamond on the chart (or convenient diamonds if there are several near your route) you know the offset distance. When sailing cross-tide, do not try to stem the tide unless it is in one direction for the entire projected length of the leg. Work out the net effect from the diamonds and allow the offset in the opposite direction. Stemming the tide reduces forward speed. Let the tide carry you up and down and aim for the offset point!

4 When the wind dies (or strengthens) the estimated time of arrival is altered. If this is a significant change, a new offset from where you are to the mark should be calculated and the course adjusted accordingly. Remember to navigate from where you *are* and not from where you should be.

5 As the wind got lighter towards the French coast it was important to make westerly distance by using the last of the west-going tide, in spite of the fact that tacking onto port at this time meant losing a lee-bow on starboard. The tides run very

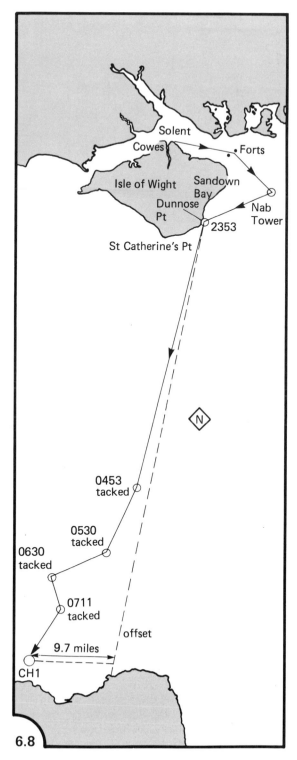

6.8

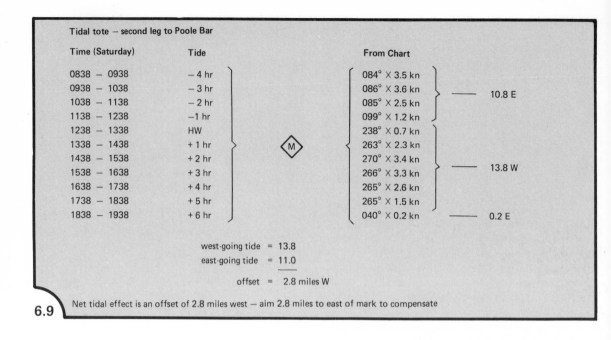

Tidal tote – second leg to Poole Bar

Time (Saturday)	Tide		From Chart	
0838 – 0938	– 4 hr		084° X 3.5 kn	
0938 – 1038	– 3 hr		086° X 3.6 kn	
1038 – 1138	– 2 hr		085° X 2.5 kn	10.8 E
1138 – 1238	–1 hr		099° X 1.2 kn	
1238 – 1338	HW	M	238° X 0.7 kn	
1338 – 1438	+ 1 hr		263° X 2.3 kn	
1438 – 1538	+ 2 hr		270° X 3.4 kn	
1538 – 1638	+ 3 hr		266° X 3.3 kn	13.8 W
1638 – 1738	+ 4 hr		265° X 2.6 kn	
1738 – 1838	+ 5 hr		265° X 1.5 kn	
1838 – 1938	+ 6 hr		040° X 0.2 kn	0.2 E

west-going tide = 13.8
east-going tide = 11.0

offset = 2.8 miles W

6.9 Net tidal effect is an offset of 2.8 miles west – aim 2.8 miles to east of mark to compensate

strongly off Cherbourg at springs, and to be downtide of CH1 buoy in light airs would be to lose the race.

6 Always look into the possibility of tidal gates. One cannot plan a tidal gate, but being aware of its existence does help in planning the succeeding stages of the race, and it also helps crew morale enormously if they know about it.

Rounding CH1

'Yeoman' rounded CH1 buoy about 15 minutes ahead of the next Class 1 boat. The wind was very light at this time and so the distance between the boats was only about three-quarters of a mile. The tactics of most of the fleet had been similar for the run across and so there were no very large gaps between the boats. In other words we were in a good but not necessarily a winning position. The real lesson from this race in terms of tidal tactics came on the second leg to Poole Bar buoy.

The second leg

After clearing CH1 the tide began running to the east very strongly. This can be seen by reference to the tidal tote on the way back (figure 6.9). This was compiled with reference to tidal diamond M

which was in the middle of the rhumb line back to Poole Bar buoy on a magnetic course of 358 degrees. The wind was southerly backing to SSE at about 10 knots. To gain any speed at all, boats would have to put the wind on their quarter and gybe downwind. The question was, which gybe? We chose the starboard gybe as shown in figure 6.10. With the tide pressing on our port beam and effectively pushing the boat into the wind, the apparent wind was increased. To our surprise, boats following us round CH1 (with the exception of the Class 1 yacht 'Nick-Nack' which eventually came second) went away from the mark on port gybe. Our initial heading was 020 degrees. Most of the fleet went away on about 315 degrees of port gybe. This meant that not only were they stemming the east-going tide (figure 6.10) but the wind over their deck was being lessened by a component of the tidal stream – in other words they were being pushed away from the wind.

By 1150 the wind had backed to the south-east and, still remaining on starboard gybe, we were able to alter course to port to 355 degrees magnetic, with the tide still running to the east. When we finally gybed at 1345, just after the turn of the tide, we were fifteen miles to the east of the rhumb line.

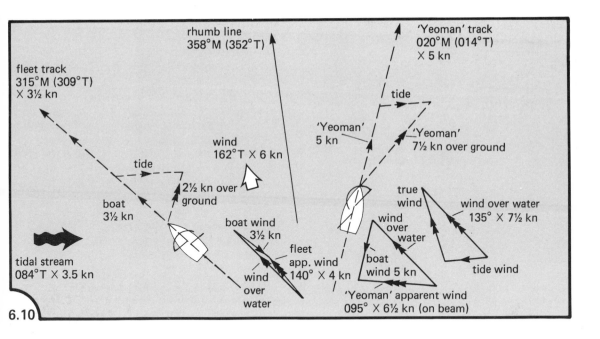

6.10

As soon as we gybed onto port the tide, which was now westerly and on our starboard beam, began to push us into the wind again increasing our apparent wind. We made good progress from 1345 onwards, steering a course of 315 degrees magnetic and actually making good over the ground a course of about 300 degrees magnetic. At about 1600 we crossed the rhumb line without any sign of the fleet (giving rise to great feelings of pessimism amongst the skipper and crew, stoutly resisted by the navigator) until we reached the position shown in figure 6.11 for 1638 on Saturday afternoon. At this point we gybed again onto starboard on a course of approximately 020 degrees, although because of the west-going tide we only made good over the ground 358 degrees magnetic. As can be seen from figure 6.9 the tide turns at diamond M at about 1830. By this time we were off the coast near Anvil Point, and since the tide turns first inshore, 'Yeoman' was pushed round the point towards Poole Bar buoy, which we rounded at 1925. Course was then set for St Catherine's Point; with the increasing flood tide behind us, and the wind just forward of the beam and increased in velocity by the boatspeed and the favourable tidal stream, we made good speed.

After we had left Poole Bar buoy four or five miles behind, one solitary sail could be seen on the horizon on the starboard quarter which we identified as 'Nick-Nack'. She was about eight miles astern of us at that stage; unbeknown to us she was leading the rest of the fleet by another eight or nine miles, since they had drifted out to the west and what wind they had was reduced to almost nothing by the adverse effect of this downtide drift on their apparent wind. The navigator was confident that we were leading the fleet, but the skipper and crew kept a sharp look-out ahead for the walking wounded of Class 5!

Because the rest of the fleet was so far astern, another tidal gate was experienced at St Catherine's Point. 'Yeoman' rounded St Catherine's Point with a strong favourable tide and then Bembridge Ledge buoy, which marks the easternmost shoal off the Isle of Wight, at 0015 on the morning of Sunday 15th. At high water Portsmouth (0138 on that morning) the tide begins to run both into the Solent and around the outer side of the Isle of Wight and down the Channel in a westerly direction. All the boats heading east from Poole Bar buoy and trying to round St Catherine's were thus faced with an

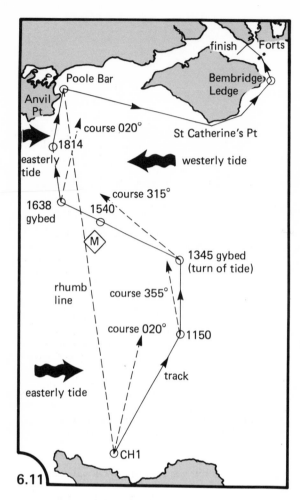

finish   Forts

Poole Bar

Bembridge
Ledge

Anvil
Pt.

course 020°

St Catherine's Pt

1814

easterly
tide

westerly tide

course 315°

1638
gybed

1540

M

1345 gybed
(turn of tide)

rhumb
line

course 355°

course 020°

1150

track

easterly tide

CH1

6.11

point of this race was a correct appreciation of
tidal strategy on the second leg, and the
coincidental opening of tidal gates for the lead
boat after a big gap had been established between
'Yeoman XXIII' and the rest of the fleet.

Conclusion

There is really one conclusion to be drawn, and
that is that you must have a very clear idea of
tidal strategy and what the juxtaposition of light
winds and big tidal streams will do to the boat.
Enormous gains can be made if this strategy can
be correctly appreciated.

Offshore racing and the tide

Tidal streams are on offer, free, like the wind.
Sometimes they oppose and sometimes they
assist, and more often than not their offer of
assistance is ignored.

You must know which way your boat is going
over the ground. Use your Decca or Loran set
with the current position set at zero, as a waypoint.
As the boat moves a bearing will come up on the
screen; this will be the bearing to the waypoint
(your former position), and will be the reciprocal
of the direction in which your boat is moving.
You may need to kedge. Do not trust wavering
bearings of hills or objects ten miles off taken
with a hand-bearing compass. Use your electronic
instruments, since they are usually sensitive to
movements of 20 yards or so. Some boats can
drift back three-quarters of a mile while people
on deck argue about bearings and decide whether
or not to kedge.

An enormous amount of research has gone into
making the best of the wind, and many books
have been written on the subject and are avidly
read by the sailing fraternity. Research into
making the best of tidal streams and currents has
tended to lag behind; and yet tidal streams can
regularly be over half the hull speed of the average
racing yacht in non-enclosed waters, and can very
often mean the difference between winning and
losing. I hope that this book will go some way
towards redressing the balance.

adverse tide. 'Yeoman', having rounded
Bembridge Ledge at high water, had the first of
the ebb pushing her westward through the Forts,
and to the Fort Gilkicker finish at 0108 on Sunday
morning.

'Nick-Nack', the boat that was second overall
and the only other boat to follow us to the east on
the second leg across, came second, finishing
some two and half hours after us. Twelve hours
later, Class 1 boats were still finishing. The pivotal

7 Tide facts

This chapter, although not essential to an understanding of sailing tactics in tidal waters, gives a background to the causes of tides, why they vary in duration, why they change in period in various parts of the earth, and what causes all these variations. You will find it much easier to look up tides and to understand the results you get if you have some knowledge of the factors that go towards determining the tide at any one place at any one time.

Causes of tides
Tides are caused by the attraction of the moon and the sun. The moon being closer causes a greater attraction, even though the sun is of a greater mass. On average the sun has about three-sevenths the effect of the moon (i.e. about 42 per cent of the effect).

Newton's law
Newton explained the connection between the moon, the sun and the tidal effect. Newton's law states that the gravitational force between two bodies is proportional to their mass and inversely proportional to the square of the distance between them. Since the sun is much further away from the earth than the moon, this is the reason why it has less effect than the moon on the earth's tides.

The important part of Newton's law is the fact that the force lessens by the square of the distance. In figure 7.1 object A attracts object B with a force x. Object C is twice as far from A as object B. If A, B, and C are of equal mass, the attractive force on C is $x/4$. In other words, doubling the distance reduces the force to a quarter. This is the inverse square rule.

In figure 7.2 a line has drawn showing where the force on an object would be $x/2$ (the average of the forces on B and C). Let's call this the average force line.

Now look at figure 7.3 and imagine that object A is the moon and object B is on the nearside of the earth, with a force x attracting it to the moon. Simplifying a bit, if object C is on the far side of the earth then it will only be attracted towards the moon with a quarter the force.

The average force line is also shown in figure 7.3; on this line the pull on an object would be $x/2$ Note that the line goes through the north and south poles. It is useful to imagine that B has a *positive* force towards the moon relative to the average force, while C has a *negative* force relative to the average. Indeed, all objects in the white area will have a positive force towards the moon, while all those in the grey area will have a negative force.

It is the difference in gravitational force between points on the earth that gives rise to tides, as we shall now see.

Applying Newton's law to the sea around the earth
First of all it is convenient to imagine the earth with an envelope of water all around it, unimpeded by any land mass and spinning once every 24 hours on its north/south

7.1

force $x/4$ — C
force x — B ... A

1 unit | 1 unit

7.2

C $x/4$
B x
A
average force line

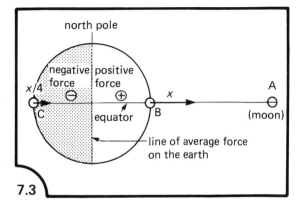

7.3

north pole

negative force $x/4$ positive force

C

equator B x A (moon)

line of average force on the earth

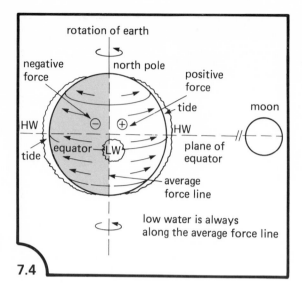

rotation of earth

negative force

north pole

positive force

tide

moon

HW

HW

tide

equator — LW

plane of equator

average force line

low water is always along the average force line

7.4

axis with the moon on a line parallel to the plane of the equator. This is shown in figure 7.4.

The average force line corresponds to the axis of spin. Water particles to the right of this (near the moon) will be pulled towards the moon, while water particles to the left (in the grey area) experience negative forces and are pulled away from the moon. The result is a tidal surge (or bump, if you like) on the side of the earth nearest the moon, and another 'bump' on the side of the earth furthest away from the moon. These are the two high tides at any instant, and corresponding low tides are experienced on each side of the earth (level with the spin axis in this case) where only the average force is acting. The tidal surges move with the moon as it circles the earth.

The earh spins once every 24 hours, and an observer at one fixed spot would be carried around with it and would experience two high tides and two low tides in the day. This is known as a *semi-diurnal* tide. It is the rotation of the earth that causes the oscillation of the tides. Without rotation there would simply be a slight bump in the water surface on each side of the earth, but this would be stationary and of negligible effect.

The actual pull of the moon is only about one millionth that of gravity. For this reason (and contrary to popular belief) vertical pull does *not* affect the tides significantly. Tides are caused by a horizontal pulling force which follows the moon around. When the moon rises the pull is to the east, and when it sets it is to the west.

The effect of the sun
The effect of the sun is similar, although it acts with less power than the moon. The main importance of the

sun is its effect of either reinforcing the moon's force or reducing it, which gives rise to *spring tides* and *neap tides*. Remember that spring tides are tides that have higher 'high water' and lower 'low waters' (i.e. the greatest range). Neap tides have lower 'high waters' and 'higher 'low waters' (i.e. the smallest range). How this comes about is shown in figures 7.5 to 7.7.

In figure 7.5, with the bright side of the moon towards the sun and away from the earth (new moon), it can be seen that the pull of the moon and of the sun act together (conjunction) and a higher than usual tide will result. This gives us the spring tides. In figure 7.6 the bright side of the moon is towards the earth (full moon) but the moon and sun are still in conjunction since they are still pulling the two high tides on either side of the earth. This also gives rise to spring tides.

In figure 7.7 the moon and sun are in opposition. This situation occurs when half the moon is visible (in figure the moon is waning, i.e. disappearing towards a new moon). Were the moon to be waxing on the opposite side of the earth to that shown, the same effect would occur. This causes the neap tides which, when the moon is waning, occur approximately 22 degrees in front of the line connecting the earth and the moon.

In figure 7.7 the tide is 'leading' because it is ahead of the moon due to the resultant pull of the sun and the moon. When the moon is waxing (i.e. below the earth on our figure) the tide 'lags' 22 degrees behind the moon's path, and is also a neap tide. In intermediate situations between opposition and conjunction of the sun and the moon, the range of the tide either grows towards springs (conjunction) or reduces towards neaps (opposition).

The moon revolves around the earth every 29½ days on average. In this time it is twice in conjunction with the sun and twice in opposition, giving two spring tides and two neap tides every 29½ days. The effect of this is that one week has a spring tide in it, the next week has a neap tide in it, and so on. In other words, when there is a new moon or a full moon, spring tides can be expected. When half the moon is visible, neap tides can be expected.

One way of predicting the approximate time of high tide is to add 50 minutes to the time of high tide the previous day. This holds roughly true on the semi-diurnal cycle described above throughout the whole 29-day cycle of the moon.

Declination tides
So far we have only considered the earth covered with a uniform envelope of water and the moon (or the sun) facing at right angles to the axis of spin. *Declination* is the angle between the plane of the equator (which is at right angles to the axis of spin) and the line from the centre of the earth to the moon (or the sun). Because of its much greater effect on tides in general, it is convenient to consider only the effect of the moon's

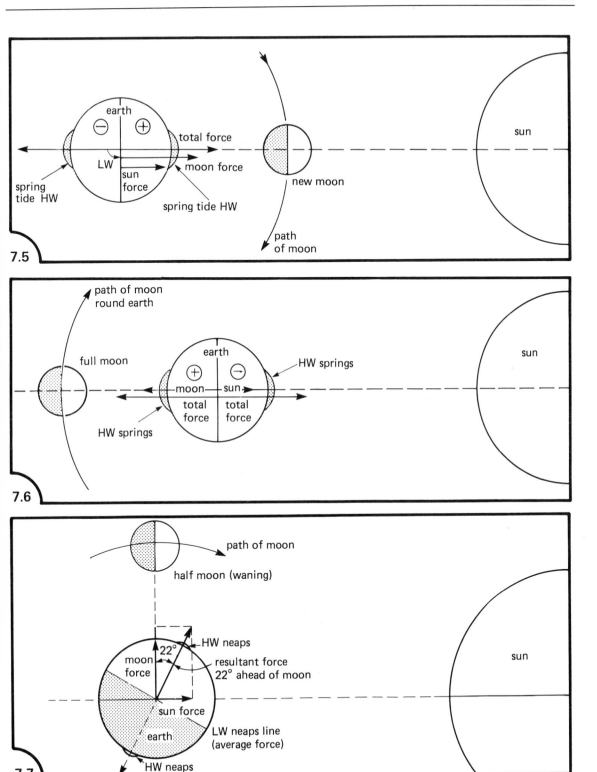

7.5

7.6

7.7

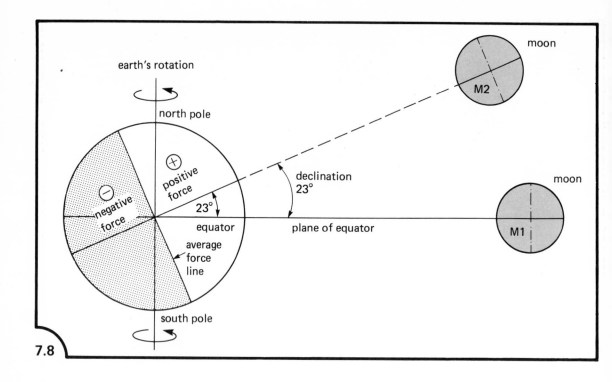

earth's rotation

north pole

positive force

⊕

negative force

⊖

equator

23°

declination 23°

plane of equator

average force line

south pole

7.8

moon

M2

moon

M1

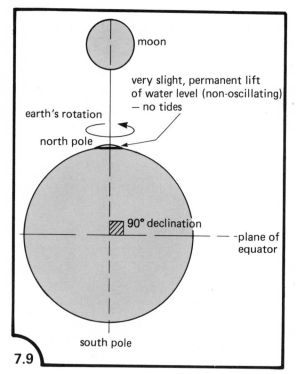

moon

very slight, permanent lift of water level (non-oscillating) – no tides

earth's rotation

north pole

90° declination

plane of equator

south pole

7.9

declination here, although the same effect would be experienced with the sun to a lesser extent.

The moon and the sun only travel up and down from about 23 degrees north of the equator to 23 degrees south of the equator, and this is shown in figure 7.8. Note that in this figure we are looking at the earth in side view – in the previous figures we were 'looking down' on the north pole.

To see more clearly the effect of declination on the tidal effect let's look at an extreme (and impossible) case: in figure 7.9 the moon has a 90-degree declination, i.e. it is situated over the north pole. All that would happen here is that the gravitational effect would cause lifting of the water envelope on the earth's surface under the moon, but there would be no tide at all since as the earth spins there would be no change in the moon's position relative to the earth – it would remain stationary over the north pole. It follows from this that the tidal effect of the moon (and the sun for that matter) is maximum when it is on the plane of the equator and reduces progressively to zero when it is over the pole (if it could ever be in that position).

The immediate effect of moving the moon from the plane of the equator (M1 in figure 7.8) to a declination of 23 degrees north (M2) is to rotate the line of average force away from the axis on which the earth spins. The grey area contains the negative forces (further away from the moon than the average force line) and the

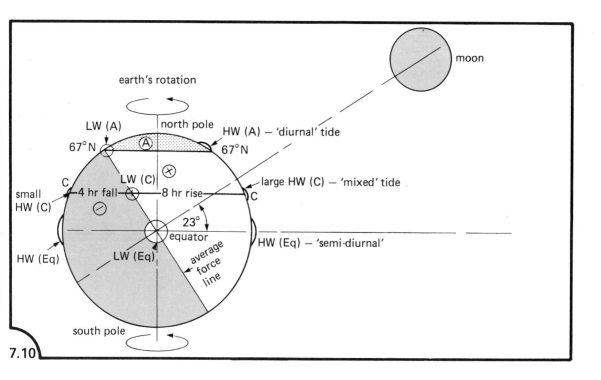

7.10

white area has the positive forces (nearer to the moon than the average force line). Remember that the tides follow the change in the moon's position and not the spin line of the earth.

From this a rule can be formulated – *the more the declination, the less the tidal effect*. However, other effects come into play (as shown in figure 7.10) when declination is taken into account.

Figure 7.10 is a slightly amplified version of figure 7.8 with the moon at 23 degrees north declination. It so happens that at a latitude of 67 degrees north (90 degrees minus declination) the moon is above the horizon all the time. This is shown in area A. You will note that all of area A is to the positive side of the average force line, which itself is at right angles to the direction of the moon – as one might expect, since it is the line of equal distance from the moon to the earth's surface. The earth, however, spins around the north pole and so only that part of area A closest to the moon experiences a high tide. In area A there are no negative forces, so low water is experienced on the other side of area A, and a sailor in area A at a fixed point will only experience *one* high water and one low water each 24 hours. Were the earth to be completely covered in water without any intervening land masses this type of tide would be experienced in high latitudes when the moon and the sun were at their maximum declinations. This is known as a *diurnal* tide.

Meanwhile on the equator, where the spin axis between the north and south poles coincides with the average force line, the same old semi-diurnal tides persist.

The interesting area to consider is that marked by line C, somewhere between the equator and 67 degrees north. Some of the time the gravitational force is positive (i.e. in the white area), but for part of the day the force is negative (in the grey area, to the left of the average force line). What this gives is a mixed diurnal and semi-diurnal tide – an example of which would be eight hours rise of tide to high tide; eight hours fall of tide to low tide; four hours rise of tide to a small high tide; and four hours fall of tide to a small low tide. This is known as a mixed tide.

Effect of land masses
The earth is not, of course, a perfect sphere covered with an unbroken blanket of water. Geographic effects of bays, islands, rivers, headlands and continents modify the tides from the pattern which could be predicted from a consideration of the movement of the sun and the moon and declination. Nonetheless, areas such as the Australian coast and the west coast of America experience mixed tides in varying degrees while other (admittedly rather rare) areas experience at times pure diurnal (24-hour) tides when the

declination of the moon and/or the sun is at a maximum in that hemisphere.

Distance of the sun and the moon from earth

Newton's law states that the attraction of two bodies varies inversely with the square of their distance apart. Both the moon and the sun vary their distance from the earth. The sun is nearest the earth in December each year and furthest from the earth in June each year, but the effect of this is small. The moon varies in its distance rather more frequently from approximately 250,000 miles away (the *apogee*) to approximately 230,000 miles away (the *perigee*). When the moon is closest to the earth, at spring tides an extra-high tide is generated known as *perigee springs* (Remember: **a**pogee – **a**part.)

Summary

- The main tidal generating effect is a horizontal force causing a surge of water, and this follows the path of the moon across the heavens (and to a lesser extent the path of the sun). A similar surge is generated on the other side of the earth.
- The force is greater when the moon and sun are in conjunction, which gives spring tides. It is least when the moon and sun are in opposition, which gives neap tides.
- The force is greater when the moon and sun are at zero latitudes (i.e. on the plane of the equator) which occurs generally in March and September.
- The force is greater when the moon (or the sun) is nearest the earth. This gives perigee springs.
- Were there to be no land, the maximum tide would be felt on the equator and the tide would be zero at the poles. This is because the difference of distance from the moon to opposite sides of the earth is greatest where the earth is at its thickest (i.e. the equator) and diminishes to zero at the pole (see Newton's law above). Tide is, however, subject to geographic effects and the largest tides do not occur at the equator in practice.

- The moon is the dominant influence on tidal forces, with the sun providing on average about 42 per cent of the lunar force. Nonetheless, in different parts of the world the solar tide effect varies from 6 per cent of the lunar effect to 100 per cent of the lunar effect (i.e. the two bodies have equal effect in some places).

- In most equatorial temperate latitudes, the tides are semi-diurnal (i.e. two high waters and two low waters every day). In some areas due to the geographic effects mentioned above and at high latitudes, the tides are sometimes diurnal (one tide every 24 hours when the moon is at its maximum declination). The higher the latitude north or south, the more likely it is that there will be a dominant tide over a longer period (i.e. when the moon is above the horizon at the place concerned) and a smaller tide over a shorter period (when the moon is below the horizon). This is a mixture of a diurnal and semi-diurnal effect and is known as a mixed tide.

This is a simplified description of the cause and effect of the moon and the sun on tides, but it contains all that needs to be known by a sailboat tactician.

The SAIL TO WIN series

Tactics   *Rodney Pattisson*
Dinghy Helming   *Lawrie Smith*
Dinghy Crewing   *Julian Brooke-Houghton*
Wind Strategy   *David Houghton*
Tuning your Dinghy   *Lawrie Smith*
The Rules in Practice   *Bryan Willis*
Boatspeed: Supercharging your Hull, Foils and Gear   *Rodney Pattisson*

published by Fernhurst Books